HUMAN RESOURCE MANAGEMENT AND DEVELOPMENT

Human Resource Management and Development

Current Issues and Themes

John Kempton

First published 1995 by
MACMILLAN PRESS LTD
Houndmills, Basingstoke, Hampshire RG21 6XS
and London
Companies and representatives
throughout the world

ISBN 0–333–60158–0

A catalogue record for this book is available from the British Library.

10   9   8   7   6   5   4   3
04   03   02   01   00   99   98   97

Printed in Great Britain by
Antony Rowe Ltd
Chippenham, Wiltshire

Published in the United States of America 1995 by
ST. MARTIN'S PRESS, INC.,
Scholarly and Reference Division
175 Fifth Avenue, New York, N.Y. 10010

ISBN 0–312–12597–6

To Amanda, Eleanor, Sarah, Frank and especially Pat

'my critics jumped and shouted'

Contents

vii

Introduction

The management of the human resource is not an exact science. Our knowledge of how organisations and people work is not complete. The purpose of this book is to try to explain a little about what goes on in organisations. That is, to take some of the complicated theories and ideas to see whether they really work or are relevant. One of the important points to remember is a word of warning from Brecht in *Mother Courage*: 'The finest plans have always been spoiled by the littleness of them that should carry them out.'

Porter, Lawler and Hackman (1975) in their work on organisation change suggest that there are three perspectives to viewing organisations: as a whole; as a collection of groups or teams; as a collection of individuals.The ideas and theories of individuals and organisations will be assessed against these three categories.

I make my living as a training and organisation development consultant. What that means is that I help organisations to decide what they want to achieve and/or how to improve what they are doing. As part of this process I deliver a lot of training across the spectrum of human resource management. I am also a lecturer in personnel and management for institutions such as the Civil Service College and the University of Surrey. My experience in education and in the world of work has led me to write this book.

I attempt to pick out some of the key theories in management to show just what they mean for organisations and the people who work in them.

The book starts by detailing the framework within which we live and work. Part I, then, is about *understanding the principles.* Chapters 1 and 2 look at what makes organisations work, starting with a look at theories of organisation and how they affect the structure of organisations. Chapter 2 looks at the people who make organisations work and then moves on to examine how people are different and what motivates them.

Having established the base to work upon and some of the practices that go on in organisations, in Part II we look at *organisational necessities,* that is what organisations are trying to achieve and what is 'good practice' in areas such as compensation and benefits (Chapter 3) and recruitment and selection (Chapter 4). Chapter 5 will examine some other important human resource management practices, such as manpower planning and communication. The final chapter in Part II examines practices in training and development.

Part III is concerned with *good organisational practices* and examines some of the practices that have major effects on the way the organisation works. Topics discussed are leadership (Chapter 7), performance management and assertiveness (Chapter 8) and counselling (Chapter 9).

Part IV is the final section and looks at *making the ideal organisation*. That is, looking at how the organisation could be, and can be. Chapter 10 explores change, in particular change management, quality and customer care. The final chapter (Chapter 11) concentrates on empowerment, an approach that can incorporate all the good ways of operating to meet the needs of both individuals and the organisation.

JOHN KEMPTON

Acknowledgements

The author and publishers are grateful to the following for permission to reproduce copyright material: Prentice-Hall for material from David A. Kolb, *Experiential Learning*; Simon & Schuster for material from Gray and Starke, *Organization Behavior*; Gower for material from John Adair, *Action-Centred Leadership*; Blackwell Publishers for material from D. Pym in an article in *Journal of Management Studies*, 3 (1986); *Management Today* for material from C. Clarke and S. Pratt in an article in *Management Today*, March 1985; Scientific Methods for the Leadership Grid material (see page 143); Kogan Page for material from M. Armstrong, *A Handbook of Personnel Management*; Random House for material from Charles Handy, *The Age of Unreason*; *Personnel Management* for material from 'Why companies review performance' in *Factsheet 3 March 1988 on Performance Appraisal*; *Harvard Business Review* for material from R. Tannenbaum and W. Schmidt in an article of May/June 1973. Every effort has been made to contact all the copyright-holders, but if any have been inadvertently omitted the publishers will be pleased to make the necessary arrangement at the earliest opportunity.

Part I

Understanding the Principles

1 The Foundations of the Organisation

This chapter is the first in the section entitled 'Understanding the Principles'. Part of the process of understanding the principles is to develop an understanding of the foundations of the organisation, so the place to start is with organisation theory and organisation structure.

Organisation theory provides a framework for understanding organisations. With it we can try to predict what certain kinds of organisation will do in different situations. It also helps to provide models to explain what has happened, or is happening, in an attempt to try to understand the complex organisations that we work for, interact with and live with.

Let me give you an example. One day in June 1994 I was sitting in my office trying to finish this book when a large swarm of bees appeared in my garden and settled 30 foot up on the branches of a large hawthorn tree. Fascinating as it was to have these bees, for the safety of my young children – who usually play in the garden – I thought I should have them removed.

I called an expert, a beekeeper, who – for a small fee – offered to take them away. The beekeeper put on his protective clothing and got his equipment ready. He advised me that the way to catch a swarm is to trap the queen and put her in a temporary hive. All the other bees will follow her and move from the tree (or the air) to be with her. After several attempts the beekeeper felt confident that he had caught the queen. Sure enough, by the evening all the bees had gone into the temporary hive, which was then removed.

There are many lessons we could learn from this tale but the key one I wish to put over is that the beekeeper had a good knowledge of bees and knew all he had to do was to find the queen and the rest would follow. He was able to predict fairly accurately the behaviour of the bee swarm, based on his knowledge of how other bees behave in similar circumstances. A comparable knowledge of organisations could enable us to understand and even predict what is happening in organisations. I could go on to describe management consultants (some of them anyway) as the beekeepers of organisations, but maybe that is pushing it a bit far.

ORGANISATION THEORY

In the development of our understanding of organisation theory it is useful to look at the key approaches:

● Pre-classical
● Classical theory
● The human relations approach
● The systems approach
● Contingency theory
● Social action

Pre-Classical

There is a link between organisation and civilisation. The Greeks were very well organised – mostly into citizens and slaves! The Roman Empire was also achieved by being organised. Its success is normally attributed to its army – organised into legions with centurions.

Modern theories of organisation arose from the Industrial Revolution, which introduced factories and therefore organisation of man and resources. There was however little systematic organisation, indeed it can be suggested that factory workers were required to use less skill than they had previously used on the land.

Adam Smith and Karl Marx both proposed that simplification 'beyond a certain point' could have diminishing returns and produce feelings of alienation in workers.

Classical Theory

This first approach to management theory looked at the organisation in terms of its purpose and structure. Emphasis was placed on the planning of work. Assumptions were also made that people behaved in a rational, logical way.

The assumption of classical theory was that it was possible to work out the best way to do a job and then fix that forever. A legacy of this approach is 'time and motion' study, where trained observers observe a process such as a production line and fix the standards of required performance. What this approach forgets, of course, is the human element!

Another example of where classical theory hinders organisations is where they have very detailed instructions on how to perform tasks. It may be that in certain environments, such as a plastics factory, this kind of proscribed approach is necessary – but translate it to a utility such as British Gas or to a shop dealing with customers and it may not be appropriate. The standards and instructions that are in place cannot hope to deal with every eventuality.

Logically we can understand that there is often (if not always) at least one other way of achieving the right result. An outcome of this organisation system is the process of 'quality circles', an idea borrowed from Japanese management whereby work teams are taken away from the job and encouraged to think of different and better ways of performing their tasks.

The chief exponent of the 'scientific management' approach was an American – Frederick W. Taylor (1947). His main research was conducted at the Bethlehem Steel works in 1911. Taylor started by observing a carefully selected man called Schmidt whose job was to move 100 pound blocks of pig iron onto a railroad carriage from a loading bay. Taylor analysed the work involved and broke it down to its constituent parts. That is, how many blocks could the man carry at once, how far did he have to move them and so on. Taylor then set the *optimal level of mechanical efficiency*. With this new approach Schmidt achieved a consistently higher level of efficiency. Indeed his improvement in productivity was 280 per cent

To support the extra effort Taylor introduced a performance related pay scheme to reward people for their extra effort. This idea has certainly stayed with us. Taylor, though, decided to limit the pay scheme to a maximum wage increase of 60 per cent regardless of how much worker productivity increased.

Scientific management suited the culture of its day, which was one of increasing productivity and a strong belief in the usefulness of 'science' and scientific methods. Some of the ideas are still upheld, notably that complex tasks can be broken down into simple functions and the process, therefore, is more easily controlled. However scientific management declined. One of the most important reasons for this was the role of people in organisations. As work increased in complexity so the workforce needed to be more specialised and flexible.

Some of the problems associated with this approach are:

1. It can be very costly, in terms of time and money, to establish systems and maintain them.
2. Workers can often be resistant to being observed and 'slow down'.
3. The type of work produced is of the production line variety. Therefore workers may from time to time throw the proverbial spanner in the works to produce a reaction of stopping the process or producing some variety into a monotonous job. One of the best examples of a stereotype produced by the production line is that of Charlie Chaplin in the film *Modern Times*.

Henri Fayol

Henri Fayol (1841–1925, see Fayol, 1949) was a French industrialist and theorist. He developed his ideas of management at the same time as Taylor. It is assumed that neither knew of the other's existence and work. Fayol, in his book published in 1916, defines the role of management as follows: 'to manage is to forecast and plan, to organise, to command, to coordinate and to control'.

Fayol also devised 14 'principles of management' that describe organisations in a very rigid and unchanging way. Classical theory views organisations as being predictable and in many ways paternalistic. Fayol's principles of management (see Cole, 1990) are:

1. *Division of work*: dividing the work reduces the span of attention or effort for any one person or group. It develops practice and familiarity.
2. *Authority*: managers have the right to give orders. However authority should not be considered without reference to responsibility.
3. *Discipline*: the outward mark of respect in accordance with formal or informal agreements between the firm and its employees.
4. *Unity of command*: one man one boss.
5. *Unity of direction*: one leader and one plan for a group of activities with the same objective
6. *Subordination of individual interests to the general interest*: the interests of one individual or group should not prevail over the general good.
7. *Remuneration*: pay should be fair to both the employee and the firm.

8. *Centralisation*: centralisation will always be present to a greater or lesser extent, depending on the size of the organisation and the quality of its managers.
9. *Scalar chain*: a line of authority from the top to the bottom of the organisation.
10. *Order*: a place for everything and everything in its place, the right man in the right place.
11. *Equity*: a combination of kindliness and justice towards employees.
12. *Stability of tenure of personnel*: employees need to be given time to settle into their jobs, even though this may be a lengthy period in the case of managers.
13. *Initiative*: within the limits of authority and discipline, all levels of staff should be encouraged to show initiative.
14. *Esprit de corps*: harmony is a great strength to an organisation; teamwork should be encouraged.

Later in this chapter I will compare this list of classical ideas with the current practices of contingency theory.

This description by Fayol reads all too much like the practices in place in many organisations in the UK and abroad today. In many ways one can see why senior managers want to run organisations along paternalistic, almost military lines – it is because they think they are in control of the people and the process.

The training manager at a city bank that is moving to the 'Docklands' development told me how it should be possible for many of the staff to work from home as required: the technology of PCs, faxes and phone lines is available; all the staff are closely managed in terms of their agreed objectives at appraisal interviews; and, with the dramatic reductions of staff in city institutions, staff no longer have the luxury of idle moments – so they are unlikely to be skiving! The block to working from home was the attitude of the senior managers – they feared letting people out of their sight. Would they be able to maintain their power in this kind of organisation?

The Human Relations Approach

The human relations approach developed in the late 1920s in the United States. Due to the depression, the human element in production was starting to be seen as important. The banks were throwing people off their land and the industrial employers were making people redundant. So this approach was based more on human behaviour than on mechanical ability and people started to think of organisations as human cooperative systems.

The theoretical base of the approach came from 'The Hawthorne Studies' of Elton Mayo, a psychologist (see Roethlisberger and Dickson, 1939). Mayo and his team conducted a series of studies at the Hawthorne works of the Western Electric Company in Chicago between 1927 and 1939. An earlier experiment conducted by the Hawthorne company was based on scientific management principles and was intended to ascertain the relationship between productivity and illumination. The company wanted to find the level of lighting that was optional to productivity. The researchers found that productivity increased in the sample group regardless of the level of light. They also found that production increased in the control group where no changes were being made. The findings were that as the illumination was changed – for brighter or dimmer, output rose and fell without any direct correlation to the intensity of the illumination.

The experimenters concluded that additional factors must be present so they called in Elton Mayo, a psychologist at Harvard. Mayo, and his researchers set up two groups, one a control group and the other for testing. Both groups were made up of young women. The analysis of their research showed no significant differences in efficiency between the two groups. A further experiment recorded output rising by 25 per cent when the working arrangements had not been changed. These experiments led the researchers to propose a psychological explanation.

Their conclusion, which is known as 'The Hawthorne Effect', is that the differences were in the workers being observed. The investigators had given them a new sense of their own worth, or value, by observing them. The very act of observing and taking an interest in them caused a change in their behaviour – and greater productivity.

The researchers concluded that the increases in output were internal to the girls themselves, to the attitude they now held about the work and their group. The experiment had cocooned the girls into a world of their own. The experimenters, by asking the young women for their help and cooperation in explaining the output increases, had given them a new sense of their own self-worth. Synergy had been created.

Other conclusions from this and other experiments in the studies, were as follows.

The interaction hypothesis

If employees have the opportunity to interact with each other then high morale and productivity will result. Another outcome of the interaction hypothesis is the practice of humanising the work environment, that is, allowing people to put up pictures or personalise their work area in some way. Open-plan offices are another interpretation of this. However I think the reason why some organisations favour open-plan offices is that they think they can get more people into a limited space!

Many organisations have introduced strategic coffee points to try to encourage and develop this kind of interaction.

The participation hypothesis

Significant changes in human behaviour can only be brought about if those who are expected to change are able to participate in deciding what the changes will be. This organisational principle is very popular in the 1990s, with many organisations introducing attitude surveys to see what employees think. Sadly many companies do not appreciate this point.

A byproduct of the 12 years of research at the Hawthorne works was the outcome of over 20 000 interviews. The interviews were conducted by the experimenters in a non-judgemental way, that is they mainly listened without passing judgement. They found that people welcomed the chance to talk about themselves and about work – it gave them an opportunity to let off steam. This study helped to develop counselling as a tool and helped increase management's recognition of the importance of workers' feelings and problems.

Thus the Hawthorne studies led to lasting increased productivity by humanising the work organisation.

The Systems Approach

In this approach attention is focused on the entire organisation. Indeed the organisation should be viewed both as a whole and as part of a larger environment. Change in one part of the organisation will have an effect on other parts of the organisation. As it is a system there are inputs and outputs:

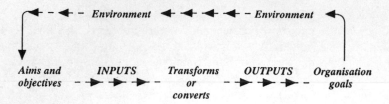

The organisation takes in (*inputs*) resources such as people, finance, raw materials and information from its environment. These are transformed or converted and returned to the environment in the form of *outputs*, such as goods or services provided, or completed processes. This achieves certain organisational goals such as profit, market-share or sales.

A current disparaging term used to describe organisational practices is 'GiGo' which reflects the systems approach to organisations as it means Garbage in–Garbage out!

One of my friends has a convertible Escort turbo. It is a lovely car … when it is going. The car left Ford in perfect working order. The problem is that a later owner had a turbo added. The car is not a factory designed turbo – the engine and other components were not designed to accommodate the extra power – and it spends a lot of time in the garage. When it is working it is excellent, but alas after three or four months it is back in for major rebuilding. This exemplifies a system that is not completed properly. The law with systems is that change in one part of the system will have an effect on another part.

One of the first studies to develop the systems approach was that of Eric Trist (1963). He developed a theory that referred to an organisation as a 'Socio-technical system'. He recognised not only that the organisation is a system but also that the social (people) and technical elements need to be in balance.

Trist, a researcher for the Tavistock Institute in London, conducted the 'Longwall Coal Mining Study', which looked into the effects of changing technology in the coalmining industry of the late 1940s. Basically miners had been used to the 'short wall' system, whereby a small group of miners would work together as an independent team. They would organise the work between them and work for each other.

The Longwall technique meant that the small teams were no longer required because new technology meant that a longer part of the seam could be worked. The researchers found, under the new system, that there was a lack of cooperation between shifts, increases in absenteeism and greater stress. Trist therefore concluded that appropriate *social* systems should be created to accompany changing *technical* systems. This would ensure that new methods would be as efficient as they could be.

What this means is that if a new system of working is set up that takes into account the social relationships at work it can be successful. Volvo in Sweden are famous for changing their car production to a system whereby seven or eight workers between them built a whole car. Instead of one worker doing the same piece of work on all cars each worker had the opportunity to do everything that goes into building one car.

Systems theory was the first approach to take an *holistic* view of the organisation.

Contingency Theory

Contingency theory can be seen as an extension of the systems approach. It is also a development on classical theory and human relations in that it proposes that there is *no* one best way. That is, there is no 'optimum state', and as each organisation is different the appropriate structure and system of management is dependent upon the 'contingencies' of the situation. Therefore each organisation will be different.

Three key studies are associated with contingency theory. Each presents a different perspective on organisations but each comes to the conclusion that organisational performance is dependent upon the degree to which the structure of the organisation matches the prevailing contingencies.

Technology
The main work on this was completed by Joan Woodward (1965), who was Professor of Industrial Sociology at Imperial College. She established a relationship between technology (or the technological process) and organisation structure. She identified three main systems of production that were increasingly more complex:

- Unit and small batch production.
- Large batch and mass production.
- Process production (such as a refinery).

In her study of 100 manufacturing companies she found that the way the company was organised reflected the system of technology used and a change in technology led to a change in the way the company was run. For example, she found that unit and small-batch companies had an average of three levels of management authority and an average span of control (number of staff supervised) of first line supervisors of 23. Process-production companies had an average six levels of management authority and first line supervisors had an average span of control of 13.

The implications to draw from this theory are that workers who are involved in one-off and small-batch production have a much greater interest in their jobs and much more involvement. They therefore require less supervision. Indeed they probably know more about their job than their supervisor does. A good example of this kind of organisation would be a Formula 1 motor racing team – a collection of specialists all working towards a common goal with few levels of management.

Environment
Burns and Stalker (1966), two British researchers, established a link between the pattern of management, the external environment and economic performance. They studied 20 Scottish industrial firms to assess their ability to change and to absorb new electronics/computer technology.

The research identified and distinguished five different kinds of environment within which these firms operated. From this they proposed the two ends of a continuum of styles. These styles would make best use of the resources in the particular situation each organisation was in. The two extremes of the continuum are 'mechanistic' and 'organic'. Mechanistic denotes rigid styles that are appropriate for stable situations; organic denotes fluid styles that are appropriate under conditions of change and uncertain environmental influences.

A mechanistic structure might be observed at a manufacturing plant. A process is set in place that has to be followed by those on 'the line'. While the external environment is stable things will run well. When there are external changes it will take a long time to introduce change.

An organic structure could be appropriate for an organisation such as a software house where changes are happening very quickly. The external environment will have a big influence on what happens.

An interesting way to think of the difference, suggested to me by one MBA student at the University of Surrey, is to think of the mechanistic approach as 'having sex' and the organic approach as 'making love'!

The Birmingham Small Arms Company, or BSA motorcycles as it is better known, is a good example of a company that operated in a very mechanistic way. It was making mainly large-capacity bikes that were (in hindsight) fairly unsophisticated. In the early 1970s the Japanese entered the marketplace with small-capacity bikes made to very high specifications. At the same time the price of petrol soared. Because BSA (and the British motorcycle industry in general) was mechanistic in approach it was not aware of the threat of competition. When realisation dawned it could not change quickly enough and went out of business.

Differentiation and integration

Lawrence and Lorsch (1967), both of the Harvard Business School, analysed organisations in terms of the differences in orientation of managers in different departments and the degree of integration between departments. This means the division of labour and specialisation *and* differences in attitude and behaviour. Integration refers to integration between departments, or even 'the quality of the state of collaboration'. (It was found to be more than just a mechanical process, as in scientific management.) They found that a lot of conflict was generated.

Their main conclusions were that the more dynamic and diverse the environment the higher the degree of differentiation and integration required. So, the more different and changeable the situation the more there is a need for specialisation and a need to get all the specialist areas working together.

They also proposed that less changeable environments require a lesser degree of differentiation but still require a high degree of integration. The third conclusion of Lawrence and Lorsch is that the more differentiated an organisation the harder it is to resolve conflict. This third conclusion is based on the observation that the more departments, divisions and specialisations within an organisation the more scope there is for conflict between the different sections to develop.

They found that the environment, in the sense of industry norms or country culture, will determine the extent of both differentiation and integration. They also suggested that a dynamic environment will produce organisations that are both highly differentiated and integrated.

These contingency theories propose that there is no one best structure for organisations. There is also no one best structure for the whole of any particular organisation. Different departments or divisions within the larger company may posses these different sub-structures.

Charles Handy, a prominent British writer and theorist, proposes a new model for organisations in his book *The Age of Unreason* (1991). This model is an attempt to define an organisational shape that can be proactive and responsive to contingencies. Handy calls this the 'shamrock' organisation'. The basic precept of this is that you have a core of workers who are highly paid, work very hard and are guaranteed continuing employment. The essential staff are supported by a vast array of contractors and part-time staff.

This model is already being adopted. Some of the organisations that I work with have only a small personnel and training department. They buy in training consultants in specialist subjects to run courses for them – they do not want, or are not big enough, to support a large number of training specialists. These same companies also have small computer departments staffed by long- and short-term contract employees. Typically they also contract security personnel from a large security

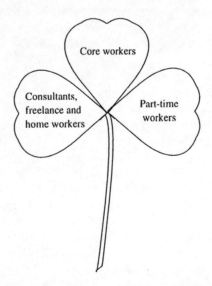

Figure 1.1   The 'shamrock' organisation

company. Other areas where external suppliers are used is in facilities management, catering, archiving and storage.

The slimmer, flatter organisation in the core is able to respond to contingencies better and more quickly. That is, they are better able to respond to difficult situations. One of the more enlightened companies that I work with went through a very difficult time recently. Revenues were down and pressure was on from head office. They responded by consulting with staff and making them an offer – if they were prepared to take on security work one day a fortnight then there would be no need for redundancies. And that's what happened – they terminated the security contract and moved some of their own staff onto security duties. Business has improved now, staff have gone back to their old jobs and a security company is back in the gatehouse.

Let us turn back to Fayol's principles of management and see how they might apply under contingency theory.

1. *Division of work*: changes from 'reduces the span of attention or effort for any one person or group; develops practice and familiarity' to 'more specialists employed with a higher level of expertise'.
2. *Authority*: changes from 'the right to give orders; a manager' to 'a leader who can inspire and be followed'.
3. *Discipline*: changes from 'outward marks of respect in accordance with formal or informal agreements between firm and employees' to 'respect is earned'.
4. *Unity of command*: changes from 'one man, one superior' to 'meeting the customers' needs'.
5. *Unity of direction*: changes from 'one head and one plan for a group of activities with the same objective' to 'meeting the customers' needs'.
6. *Subordination of individual interests to the general interest*: changes from 'the interests of one individual or group should not prevail over the general good' to 'making the general interests out of the interests of the individuals'.
7. *Remuneration*: changes from 'pay should be fair to both the employee and the firm' to 'remuneration is about more than pay'.
8. *Centralisation*: changes from 'is always present to a greater or lesser extent, depending on the size of the organisation and the quality of its managers' to 'decentralisation and empowerment'.

9. *Scalar chain*: changes from 'the line of authority from the top to the bottom of the organisation' to 'meeting the needs of the customer. Senior management helps support staff to achieve this'.
10. *Order*: changes from 'a place for everything and everything in its place; the right man in the right place' to 'no one best way'.
11. *Equity*: changes from 'a combination of kindliness and justice towards employees' to 'everyone is equal (as are suppliers and customers)'.
12. *Stability of tenure of personnel*: changes from 'employees need to be given time to settle into their jobs, even though this may be a lengthy period in the case of managers' to 'lifetime employment, training and retraining'.
13. *Initiative*: changes from 'within the limits of authority and discipline, all levels of staff should be encouraged to show initiative' to 'everyone is creative and able to show initiative'.
14. *Esprit de corps*: changes from 'harmony is a great strength to an organisation; teamwork should be encouraged' to 'mutually responsible and interdependent'.

Social Action

The most up-to-date theory on organisations is known as 'social action', which is a sociologically based theory. The theory looks at the organisation from the perspective of individual members who have their own individual goals. Work is viewed from the perspective of the satisfaction and the meaning it has for individuals. The theory is based, then, on individuals' perception of the situation and perhaps explains why conflicts of interest are seen as a normal part of organisational life. Social action is best understood as a method of analysing social relations within organisations – it is different from earlier approaches in that it deals with individual behaviour.

Fox (1966), a social action theorist, proposes two ways of looking at organisations:

1. The unitary approach: the organisation is viewed as a team with a common source of loyalty, one focus of effort and one accepted leader. Under this model conflict is explained as being a result of poor communication or personality clashes.

2. The pluralistic approach: the organisation is made up of sub-groups that are competing with each other. Therefore conflict is seen as an inevitable result of the structure of the organisation.

ORGANISATION STRUCTURE

Drucker (1974) states that 'Structure is a means for attaining the objectives and goals of an institution'. Thus organisation structure provides the framework within which organisations function.

Organisations need to establish structures that suit their needs and allow them to achieve their aims and objectives. Understanding structure helps us to analyse organisations. A structure helps an organisation to allocate the resources of time, people and technology. Internal operations such as procedures and performance objectives exist to support the aims and objectives of the organisation. The way that decisions are made will also be indicative of the structure, that is, some organisations are very slow and ponderous about making decisions while others are quick, responsive and flexible.

A leading theorist, John Child (1979), demonstrates three areas where organisation structure is visible in organisations and specifically where it assists organisations to achieve their objectives:

1. Basic structure: this is the allocation of resources and people to the tasks that have to be completed. The basic structure comprises job descriptions, organisation charts (or organograms) and the various committees or boards that run the organisation.
2. Operating mechanisms: the operating mechanisms of the structure indicate what is expected of the people in the organisation. So procedures may exist on how to complete tasks. Performance objectives will be in place for individuals (probably through performance appraisal). Objectives detailing the output or level of quality required are set and reviewed.
3. Decision mechanisms: these exist to facilitate the making of decisions and the processing of information collected from people with specialist jobs. The word that describes what decision mechanisms are all about is 'communication'.

Child proposes a contingency model of structure – that is, the structure adopted reflects the approach of the management. The preference of the decision makers for a particular style of management will be reflected in the structure. (The preference of the decision makers should be seen as their 'view of life' or 'philosophy of life'.) So, for example, Margaret Thatcher had strong views about authority and forcefulness – her cabinet was run as a clear hierarchy and those who questioned her decisions did not remain in the cabinet for long.

Alternatively, if the emphasis is placed on the importance of financial measures then accountants will be in the ascendancy. There will be a large finance department and financial control procedures will proliferate. Decisions will be made on the basis of profit and loss, and will not take into account the effect on 'human resources'.

The effects of the structure can be seen in the following areas:

- *Hierarchy*: as Joan Woodward (1965) showed there is a correlation between the number of levels in the hierarchy and the number of staff.
- *Grouping activities*, or horizontal differentiation, is how jobs are grouped together. For example this might be reflected in reporting lines, so personnel reporting into finance says something about management's view of personnel (that human resources are less important that the financial side). Other groupings could be *functional* or by *product*. Functional groupings are groupings of similar skills, so a personnel department, a finance department, a marketing department and so on. Product groupings are a mixture of skills working on one product or service. So the product team for a new computer might involve finance, manufacturing, sales, marketing and public relations.
- *Integration*. It is not uncommon for individuals and even whole departments to have differing objectives. This may be through loyalty to their own department or section but it can result in a lack of assistance. Another perspective is that actuaries have a commitment to a profession and could carry out their tasks regardless of whom their employer is. This is in stark contrast with Japanese methods of working where one becomes an employee of, say, Panasonic and does whatever job the company wants done.
- *Control*. Many management practices exist that involve control, such as budgetary control, time clocks, time and motion studies and total quality management.

When the organisation structure is inappropriate to the situation some of the following problems may be observed:

- *Motivation and morale are low.* This may occur when it is not clear who is responsible for making decisions or there are communication problems. It could also be that there are too many layers of management. Employees therefore feel they have no responsibility or decision-making authority. It could also be that there is a lack of clarity over what is expected of people.
- *Decision making is poor.* An over-extended hierarchy (one with lots of management levels) may result in information or decisions taking a long time to reach the right people. Decision makers may be overloaded because they hoard all the decisions. Another reason could be that there is no evaluation of similar decisions made in the past. In other words organisations that do not learn lessons from mistakes made in the past.
- *Conflict and lack of cooperation are present.* Conflicting objectives and priorities may exist because there is a lack of cooperation or communication is poor.
- *The organisation cannot innovate.* Senior management does not encourage, and has not put into place, mechanisms that encourage innovation and risk taking. This is clearly a problem for many organisations that are finding it hard to change. Senior managers have risen to the top by succeeding with the old ways – they have no need or desire to change the rules as they might then be at a disadvantage. A good example of this problem is an investment management company in the City of London. A collection of young managers expanded the company and took it public in the early 1970s. In the early 1990s the same half dozen managers are still in charge. New entrants to the existing elite share the same values as the managers already there. There is no incentive for the management to change.

Organisations are solutions to yesterday's problems.

Organisation Culture

An important consideration when dealing with organisation structure is the link to organisation culture. Organisation culture is evident in some of the processes of work, for example the way that power is exercised, people rewarded or laws worked out. An example of an international cultural difference is that in France it is usual for people to shake hands as a greeting the first time they meet in the morning. This practice does not take place in the UK. Charles Handy (1987) develops the work of Roger Harrison (1972) in looking at organisation structure in terms of culture; Handy proposes four cultures, these cultures or structures demonstrate the issues raised by Child (1979) in how the structures operate. The four cultures are:

- The power culture
- The role culture
- The task culture
- The person culture

The power culture

This culture depends on a single source of influence at the centre and its structure is represented by a spider's web (Figure 1.2). There is a central power source with rays of power and influence spreading out from the centre. Communication is mainly by verbal means and there are likely to be few rules and procedures. An example of this kind of culture is the communications group of Robert Maxwell. Maxwell was at the centre of a huge organisation, yet insisted on making all decisions

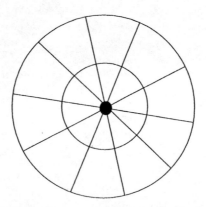

Figure 1.2   The spider's web of power

himself. The investigators into the collapsed 'empire' are still trying to untangle everything. Apparently Maxwell's personal influence extended even to authorising overtime for junior staff.

Organisations develop like this because they are able to react quickly to opportunities or threats. The power source at the centre is able to control and direct the organisation personally. It is usual to find small organisations being run in this way, but as the web gets bigger it takes more and more power to control the web. The problem with this type of organisation is that the emphasis is placed on the individual at the centre, therefore if the individual makes wrong decisions the organisation suffers. Furthermore the organisation could stagnate if that person retires, dies or leaves, creating a vacuum. This kind of culture is difficult to maintain in large structures but is quite often seen within organisations, departments or sections that are run as personal fiefdoms.

Another lovely example I read of recently is that of Richard Branson at Virgin. It seems that Branson's Range Rover turned over on the M4 motorway. Fortunately he and his family were not hurt, but the police told Branson that in any other car there would have been serious injuries. Branson has now ordered 640 Range Rovers to chauffeur Virgin's first-class passengers to Heathrow. Commendable as his actions are it shows how he is involved in every decision made at Virgin. In fact he is more than involved and makes most of the decisions. I could not help wondering what the purchasing manager thought of it all? She or he had probably spent a long time surveying the options and negotiating with Ford, Rover and others about purchasing a fleet of cars at a competitive price – and then Branson announces his decision.

This kind of structure can be described as looking like a spiders web.

The role culture

This kind of culture is often stereotyped as bureaucracy. Role culture is so-called because the roles (or positions in the organisation) are more important than the individuals who fill them. The organisation is not really interested in training and developing people into new roles. The usual response is to recruit new people. The structure of the role culture can be expressed as a Greek temple (Figure 1.3). The strength of the role organisation is in the pillars, which are the functions or specialities.

This kind of organisation can be characterised by logic and rationality. The work of the pillars and the relationships between them are

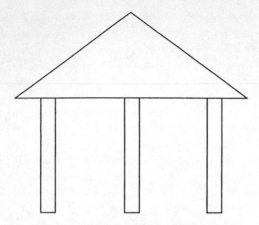

Figure 1.3   Structure of the role culture

controlled by rules and procedures. The organisation is stable and reliable and in a static environment can be very efficient. Organisations that require economies of scale rather than flexibility will have role cultures. These are probably large organisations that can offer security and predictability. Although the British Civil Service is changing we can place it into this category.

Such organisations have inbuilt inertia – making changes will be very difficult for them. Individuals performing above standard are not always desired; individuals who want to move between the pillars will not find it easy and interdisciplinary teams will be difficult to establish. Another problem is that decisions will have to go all the way up one pillar, across the top and then work its way down the next pillar. This is likely to make decision making very slow, and like an oil tanker it will be a very slow process to change direction. As already stated this type of organisation offers security and predictability and in times of change this can be a liability. Perhaps an example of an organisation that fits this stereotype is British Telecom, which is trying very hard to change the situation. The management of BT has been reducing staff levels for several years since privatisation – it is cutting out many management levels and is trying to streamline the organisation. One of its aims is multi-skilling, that is, staff are able to carry out more than one job – this is clearly an attempt to change from the restrictions of the role culture.

The task culture

This culture is job or project orientated. The organisation operates by establishing teams to manage projects autonomously. Hierarchical authority is therefore subjugated to the project or task. Handy (1987) describes the structure for this culture as being like a net (Figure 1.4). Some of the strands are thicker than others and the power and influence is located at the interstices of the net. A characteristic of the culture is that there is a high regard for experts. It is often associated with matrix structures and is dependent on the right people being brought together at the right time.

Organisations structure themselves like this (or structure part of themselves) because individuals can be highly motivated by real responsibility and will participate in projects that really matter to the organisation. Other advantages will be flexibility and speed. Individuals are allowed to contribute to key decisions and have a change from the normal routine of their jobs. This structure can work well where specialists form part of interdisciplinary teams.

Some of the disadvantages are that economies of scale are not easy to achieve, managing the project groups can be difficult and allocation of resources between the project groups can be problematic. Individuals who have been seconded to tough and demanding projects can also find it very difficult to go back to their old, more routine jobs.

Software departments and software houses are run in this way, with teams of specialists working together on specific projects. Another example could be an advertising agency, where people from different departments are assigned to a client.

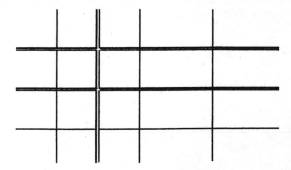

Figure 1.4   Structure of the task culture

The person culture

This culture is the least common but its values appeal to many people because the individual is the central point. The structure exists purely to serve and assist the individuals within it. The examples Handy quotes are architect partnerships, hippy communes, families and small consultancies.

Person culture is characterised by the fact that individuals can leave the organisation but the organisation seldom has the power to evict individuals. The structure is therefore minimal and is best illustrated as a cluster (Figure 1.5).

Cultures like this can take on a life beyond the personal ambition of the members. When this happens the culture can quickly change to a role or power culture. It is also possible for person culture pockets to appear in larger organisations. Computer staff in commercial companies or consultants in businesses are examples. They are, of course, difficult to manage as, being specialists, alternative employment may be fairly easy for them to find.

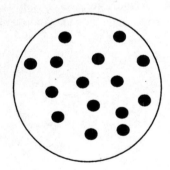

Figure 1.5   Structure of the person culture

2 The People Who Work in Organisations

This chapter concentrates on how the organisation achieves its objectives by utilising its human resources.

PERSONALITY AND INDIVIDUAL DIFFERENCES

Individuals are different. Therefore this Chapter starts by looking at what it is that makes them different. By understanding what some of the differences are, hopefully we can start to understand why individuals do some of the things they do. Indeed one of the most influential theories in the development of our understanding of organisations is the human relations approach, which places importance on human behaviour.

Individuals may be different for a variety of reasons. It may be due to their environment, how they have been brought up – usually referred to as *nurture*. Or it may be due to characteristics that an individual is born with – usually referred to as *nature*. For example, are boys born with an innate desire to play with cars and guns or is it that they pick up messages by observing others' behaviour and do what they think is expected of them – that is, adopt male stereotypes? Indeed, perhaps we could say that messages received in the womb form part of nurture – the current trend for the 'new man' and his partner is to talk to and play music to the unborn foetus.

I believe that the nature versus nurture argument will remain unresolved. Perhaps the argument is something like the philosophical debate started by Bishop Berkeley. He asked the question that if a tree fell down in a primeval forest before terrestrial animal life had evolved, did it make a sound? The debate follows that if it did make a noise there was nothing to hear the noise so can we say it made a sound?

Sociologists identify the first five years of a child's development as the 'formative' years, when they pick up most of the messages about

25

behaviour. What we can be sure of is that individuals do turn out differently, so let us look at and classify some of these areas of difference.

A list of differences relevant to human resource management, taking into account the nature versus nurture concept, might include:

- Ability
- Intelligence, or the processing of information
- How that processing is carried out
- Personality

Ability

Ability is evident in three areas: the ability to make realistic assessments of solutions to problems; the ability to be creative, to see problems from new or different viewpoints; or it can be based on social ability, the skills required to communicate and to maintain relationships.

Intelligence

Intelligence, the processing of information, can perhaps be observed in the following areas:

- Thinking
- Remembering
- Problem solving
- Evaluation

Intelligence can be measured by tests that attempt to measure (among other things) reasoning, inference, understanding and recognition. Intelligence is the ability to manage a wide variety of intellectual tasks that involve knowing and reasoning.

Many organisations carry out literacy and numeracy tests for new recruits. The practice is particularly common for graduate recruitment. The tests are an attempt to establish certain levels of ability, often in literacy and numeracy. In many cases the levels that are set for candidates are considerably higher than those exhibited by other members of staff, or higher than they will ever need to attain. It could be asked: what is the value of the formal qualifications that candidates have if they are to be ignored? Graduate recruits fresh out of university, where they have spent three years studying, are often subjected to a battery of tests like this. Is the conclusion to be drawn that degrees count for little in business, or perhaps that a degree in English literature, say, is not very relevant for business?

How Processing of Information is Carried Out

A study by Kirton (1984) looked at the way management decisions are taken, how they proceed through the organisation's decision-making structure and why they succeed or fail. Kirton proposed that there is a continuum of individual behaviour. At either end of the continuum are 'adaptors' and 'innovators'. Adaptors are people who try to modify existing systems and make them better. The innovator prefers to look at new ways of doing things.

Personality

Personality is probably the most widely used classification for identifying individual differences. Personality can be defined as the aspects of the individual that are relatively stable and enduring and distinguish one individual from another. Personality is also an aspect that allows predictions about future behaviour to be made. This definition implies two assumptions:

● That an individual's behaviour is sufficiently constant to be characteristic.
● That the idiosyncratic way in which individuals behave can be compared and contrasted.

A common approach to studying personality is to look at it in terms of traits and types.

Traits

The trait is the basis for many influential theories of personality. A trait is basically a generalisation made from observing the way a person habitually behaves in certain situations. Traits, then, are consistent responses to different circumstances. A good example of a trait is aggression. An individual can exhibit an aggressive response in a variety of situations (often inappropriate ones).

An application of trait theory is that it is used in psychometric evaluations. These evaluations attempt to determine the traits of an individual that are likely to remain constant, so that an individual's profile can be compared against the traits the organisation is looking for. For example the organisation may be looking for someone who will lead a large team. Therefore one of the traits they will be looking for is leadership.

It is worth mentioning that the British Psychological Society recommends that psychometric evaluations should not be used in isolation and that other assessment methods should be used as well. Periodically the media tells us that psychometric assessments are not worth the paper they are written on, that they are biassed and unfair. The reality comes down to how the tool is used. If it is used properly it can provide useful information to assist the decision making process. It is like the motor car. If driven carefully it provides a safe, dry mode of transport. In the hands of a 'joy-rider' it is a lethal weapon that all too often kills people (and all too frequently the teenagers doing the joy-riding).

One of the most common forms of psychometric assessment is the 16PF, developed by Cattell (1963). He proposed that there are 16 source traits (or personality factors) that can easily be identified and are relevant to the work situation. The list includes the following (showing both extremes of the dimension):

A:	Outgoing	reserved
B:	More intelligent............................	less intelligent
C:	Emotionally stable........................	affected by feelings
E:	Assertive	humble
L:	Suspicious	trusting
Q2:	Self-sufficient..............................	group-dependent
Q4:	Tense..	relaxed

A simple model of personality traits can be constructed by building on the traits identified by Jung – Introversion and Extroversion. (Jung proposed that the introvert is more interested in the inner, subjective world and the extrovert is more interested in feelings than thoughts, and in action more than fantasy) – and the factors added by Eysenck (1965) – Stable and Unstable. Below is a two-dimensional map based on these factors, forming a 'map of personality'. Eysenck also included the ancient Greek classifications of personality (shown in brackets).

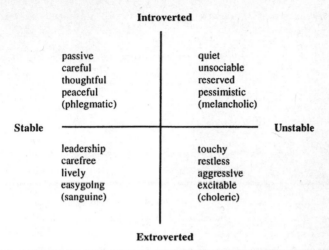

Introverted

passive	quiet
careful	unsociable
thoughtful	reserved
peaceful	pessimistic
(phlegmatic)	(melancholic)

Stable   **Unstable**

leadership	touchy
carefree	restless
lively	aggressive
easygoing	excitable
(sanguine)	(choleric)

Extroverted

To test the validity of this model try to categorise yourself and any 'famous' people you can think of (famous people tend to be stereotyped anyway). Could we say that Michael Jackson is an unstable introvert or that 'Gazza' (Paul Gascoigne) is an unstable-extrovert? Or that Sir John Harvey-Jones is a stable-extrovert?

Type

Type theories acknowledge that there are stable underlying 'traits' – it is how these interact with the properties of a particular situation that indicates a type.

Typologies based on people. One 1974 (Friedman and Rosenman) study into patients with heart disease discovered that many patients behaved in similar ways depending on whether they were type A or type B. Type A people were described as suffering from 'hurry sickness'. They had to do everything at once, and normally a number of different things at the same time. Typically, waiting in queues would be a particularly stressful activity for them. Type Bs on the other hand are people who can 'work without agitation'. They are also more able to relax. Typically type Bs are not concerned with the pressures of time urgency.

Typologies based on fluids. The earliest typology was identified by Hippocrates:

- Blood: individuals who are hopeful, confident and optimistic.
- Black bile: individuals who are melancholic and tend towards depression.
- Phlegm: individuals who are sluggish and apathetic.
- Yellow bile: individuals who are active and irascible.

Typologies based on body type. Another attempt to classify people is by their body type. Sheldon identified three basic types (although most people appear as a mix). The first is the round, soft *endomorph*, who is placid and takes pleasure in sensation. The second is the square, muscular *mesomorph*, who takes pleasure from physical activity (think of a typical prop forward and you have the type). The third is the long, thin *ecto-morph*, who is more cerebral (a recent television advertisement for Braun shows 'boffins' as tall and thin with extra large heads – the large heads might be a subconscious way of emphasising how tall and thin they are. If you have ever to been to Greece you will have noticed that all the cats look as though they have large heads, this is because their bodies are thinner than British cats and as feral cats they are not fed as well!)

Typologies based on experience patterns. Freud and his followers propose that it is childhood experiences that shape us. Thus the child is said to be 'the father of the man'. Freud even proposed three phases that the developing child has to go through, and that the individual might get 'stuck' or fixed at one of these:

- Oral: the passive, sucking type or the sadistic, or biting type.
- Anal: this behaviour is the result of severe toilet training in which the child obtains satisfaction from the control of bowel movements.
- Phallic: fixation at this stage leads to a personality that is narcissistic, exhibitionist and excessively ambitious.

Transactional analysis

In the 1960s Eric Berne (1964) developed an approach to analysing interpersonal communication based on an understanding of individual differences. Berne's work was initially in psychotherapy but it has been adapted for use in business. Transactional analysis is used to understand how people behave and how our behaviour causes others to behave.

Basically we each have a personality that has three states, known as parent, adult and child. At any given moment one state (or ego state) is in the ascendancy.

- *The child.* Our first experiences as children are remembered most as feelings. Therefore emotional outbursts or acting in an immature way are traits exhibited in this ego state. Other traits might be dependency and impulsiveness.
- *The parent.* As the child develops it learns the behaviours 'taught' by the parent. The characteristics here are authoritarianism and self-righteousness. Sometimes this state can be nurturing while at other times it can be domineering and controlling. The parent state can be subdivided further into three types of parent: nurturing parent, standard-setting parent and critical parent. This state can be said to be based on opinion.
- *The adult.* This state is not based on emotion or opinion but on logic. It can be described as information processing. The characteristics are rational thinking and mature behaviour. In the organisation an employee in this ego state will collect information and make logical decisions.

A transaction, then, originates in one of the ego states and is targeted at a particular ego state in the other person. Unfortunately the targeted person does not always respond from the desired ego state. The desired interactions in the organisational setting are adult to adult. What actually happens is that there is a lot of parent to child. The boss assumes and the subordinate complies.

Transactional analysis also introduces two other ideas: strokes and games. Strokes are expressions of praise, recognition or affection from others. When we are young this stroking is physical. As we grow older we probably need the physical stroking just as much, but as we are not so likely to receive it we make do with psychological stroking.

Games relate to the business of giving and receiving strokes. In the organisational setting we might see it in the context of managers: those in the adult state would listen attentively to a problem but those in the child state might say 'told you so'.

Transactional analysis was a popular 'fad' but some companies are starting to take it seriously again. Indeed a report in the *Independent* states that several UK law firms are providing training in it for solicitors.

The reasoning is that training in interpersonal or people skills will help solicitors to get a better result when dealing with clients and employees. 'They are like doctors who know their medicine but don't have a bedside manner'. Independent 26 March 1993

How we form impressions

The last area that needs consideration when we think about personality is the process of how we form impressions.

Human beings have a habit of forming impressions of the people they meet. They do this without the benefit of 'personality tests', so what is happening? One idea, proposed by Makin, Cooper and Cox (1991), is that we each have an implicit theory of what traits go with which, based on our own experience (and the traits we like and dislike). There are two dimensions according to which we rate people – *intellectual ability* and *sociability*. They also propose that once we have made our minds up we are loath to change our opinion! Indeed we seek information that confirms that opinion. This process is well documented by Webster (1964) in the area of selection interviewing . He suggests that decisions are made in the first three or four minutes of an interview and the rest of the interview is spent supporting that decision. Therefore, if interviewers like a candidate they might, consciously or subconsciously, ask the candidate easy questions in order to reinforce their impression. If an interviewer forms a bad first impression of you ... beware!

Makin, Cooper and Cox propose that we form instant impressions because we do not like uncertainty. Forming an impression quickly, even if it is wrong, helps to reduce uncertainty.

Attribution theory.   Attribution theory relates to the environment that we find ourselves in, and the effect it has on our actions. So, did an individual do well because of skill, expertise and judgement or was it just luck? Indeed many organisational factors such as pay, promotion or dismissal may depend upon whether attribution of responsibility is made to the situation or the person: 'She completed that excellent piece of work because she has a good degree, went to a good university and is generally very helpful.' 'He must have been helped on that project because he is normally very quiet and never makes any contribution.'

MOTIVATION

> Although many perceive its objective as disciplined obedience to a
> management plan, the real purpose of management is motivation of
> the group to use its energy to achieve objectives. (John Harvey-
> Jones, 1984)

Motivation is reflected in the attitudes and behaviour of staff.
Motivated staff exhibit high performance, energy, enthusiasm and
effort. Demotivated staff exhibit apathy, indifference and are uncooperative. Motivation theory provides an opportunity to understand the
behaviours involved.

Motivation is the process of uncovering needs and realising them.
What this means is that we each have needs or motives that we want to
fulfil. The role of management is to identify such needs and meet them
to motivate staff. So, some people are motivated by money, some by
recognition and some by doing a good job. Some people are motivated
by all these things but at different times. Motivation theory helps us to
understand what needs are and how to meet them.

An important place to start is with *assumptions about people*. Edgar
Schein (1969), an American professor, has identified some different
assumptions about people that will determine our view of how to
motivate them.

- *Rational-economic man.* This assumption is based on the work of
  Adam Smith in the 1770s and has already been referred to under
  scientific management theories. The assumption is that people are
  interested only in their own self-interests, and the 'maximisation of
  personal gain'. Schein proposes that this leads to a society of
  untrustworthy, money-oriented people being organised by a trustworthy elite – managing for the benefit of the masses. Taylor, in his
  scientific management theory, clearly stated that man is motivated
  by money. Fayol, in his classical approach, advocated a paternalistic approach from management to manage the masses.
- *Social man.* This assumption owes a lot to Mayo and the human
  relations school. The assumption is that people are motivated by
  social needs. Social interaction and groups are what people want.
  Managers who direct and control tasks are replaced by leaders who
  encourage and support.

- *Self-actualising man.* This assumption is based on a need identified by Maslow (see later in this chapter). It is not social needs that motivate people but self-fulfilment. Managers need to provide demanding and challenging work for people.
- *Complex man.* Basically people are more complicated and variable than described above. Different situations will require different approaches. So managers need to vary their own behaviour relative to that of their subordinates. The employee and the organisation need to form a 'psychological contract' based on what they expect of each other. This forms the basis of how we motivate people.

There are two key theories of motivation: content and process theories.

Content Theories

These theories tend to concentrate on the link between individual motivation and job satisfaction. They assume that needs are both physiological and psychological and that managers have the facility to offer rewards to meet individual needs.

Haslow's 'hierarchy of needs'

Probably the most influential content (and indeed motivation) theory is that of Abraham Maslow (1943) who proposes the 'hierarchy of needs', which operates on an ascending scale (Figure 2.1). As the needs at one level are met, the next level of needs is uncovered and so on until an individual reaches the highest level – self-actualisation. A person's individual motivation can also move up and down the hierarchy as a response to uncertainty or insecurity.

Physiological needs. The first level needs are concerned with having enough to eat and drink. In the organisational context this can be translated to mean physical comfort, pay and basic working conditions.

Safety needs. This level of needs, also known as security needs, is concerned with job security and avoiding redundancy.

These first two levels of need are dominant until satisfied. When satisfied the individual moves on to the higher order needs.

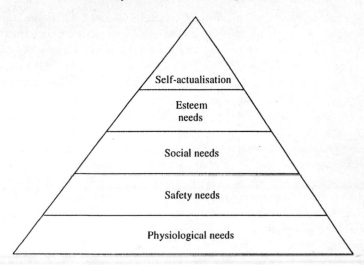

Figure 2.1   The hierarchy of needs

Social needs.   This level of need is about feeling loved and wanted. In the work situation this relates to relationships and friendships, particularly in the work group.

The next two levels of need can be thought of as being more outward facing. That is, where social needs are concerned with relationships within the organisation, the next needs are without the organisation.

Esteem needs.   This level of need is about status and recognition in the eyes of the world. The clearest interpretation of this is seen in the UK in company cars. The hierarchy is usually managed ruthlessly – junior staff cannot possibly drive the same cars as senior people. One story I heard is of a manager who was in a certain car category but wanted to be allocated the top-of-the-range model of a car in the band below. The request was vetoed by senior management because it would confuse the issue of management levels. Therefore senior management wanted it clear who was at what level! The 'I'm the king of the castle' syndrome.

Self-actualisation needs   This highest level is achieved when individuals are realising their full potential. They are completely challenged by their job and everything is absolutely great. In fact this is the target we should all be striving for, but unfortunately factors such as the job or the organisation get in the way. However if we are in the organisation that is right for ourselves, doing a job that closely matches the skills we possess, then it is possible. We might say, therefore, that the rewards are to be gained from doing the job well. The manager is a resource that helps us achieve our results.

I worked for one company where, just prior to the beginning of the recession, we had a really good thing going. Business was good, people were paid well and were well looked after. The training provided was exceptional. For a period of about six months many of us were motivated at or near the self-actualisation level. One member of staff on a training course actually said to me 'I love this company'. What he meant was, I think, that he was really motivated by the company and the people in it. And then ... recession!

Perhaps we can see some proof of Maslow's theory at the present time. People in organisations are becoming very concerned about job security, or rather fear of redundancy. It has become an overriding fear and, not surprisingly, seems to prevent people from concentrating on higher-level needs.

Hertzberg – the two-factor theory

Another approach to motivation is that of American psychologist F. Hertzberg (1959). In the 1950s he conducted a study based on questioning subjects about whether they felt especially satisfied or dissatisfied. From this he developed the 'two-factor theory'.

He identified certain needs as *satisfisers* or motivators. These factors include achievement and responsibility and the things people do at work. Hertzberg suggests that these are motivators because they are areas of personal growth.

The opposite are *dissatisfiers*. Hertzberg suggests that certain factors have to be present – and these he called hygiene factors – to prevent dissatisfaction. So a dissatisfaction was only present when a factor, such as salary, was not meeting the expectation of the employee. So, if more salary was paid the satisfaction of the employee stopped being a source of dissatisfaction, but it did not become a source of satisfaction. Most of the items identified were concerned with what is done to or for employees. The items include salary, supervision, working conditions and company policy.

The relevance of this theory for us today is that unless the job itself offers scope for personal growth then the employee will not be able to be satisfied and will therefore not be motivated. The message for organisations, then, is that you can provide excellent working conditions in an attempt to motivate staff but it is the job that needs to be exciting. Perhaps this theory can be used to explain why, if you visit the toilets (and I can only speak for the Gents) in some high-tech, prestigious companies in London and elsewhere, you will find graffiti and vandalism. You can almost hear the directors saying: 'How could the staff be so ungrateful when we provide them with these lovely open-plan offices, pot plants and glass-fronted buildings!' Every amenity for staff is provided, yet if the staff do not feel fulfilled they will not be motivated.

(The premise of this theory about fulfilling work can be found in Chapter 4. Current thinking has it that it is the managers' responsibility to make sure their staff have interesting and fulfilling tasks to complete.)

McGregor – Theory X and Theory Y

McGregor's (1960) Theory X and Theory Y are I believe two of the most influential theories of motivation because the ideas recur in other areas of human resource management. (particularly current theories on leadership and empowerment). McGregor proposed two sets of assumptions about people working in organisations.

Theory X states that people are by nature lazy and work as little as possible. They lack ambition, dislike responsibility and prefer to be led. People are also self-centred, resistant to change and indifferent to the goals of the organisation. The implications for management are that, as well as organising the elements of productive enterprise, people have to be persuaded, rewarded, punished and generally directed.

Theory Y states that people have only become passive and resistant to organisation needs as a result of their experiences in organisations. People are zestful and capable of taking responsibility. It is the responsibility of management to enable people to be able to develop themselves. The implications for management are that as well as organising the 'elements of productive enterprise' their essential task is to arrange for people to be able to achieve their own goals by directing their own performance towards the objectives of the organisation.

The kind of theory you ascribe to will flavour your views about people in organisations. Content theories concentrate on the 'content' of motivation in the form of fundamental human needs. The content theories listed above can be criticised for being very static. One way of describing content theory is to think of it as putting the cart before the horse by arguing that enhancing human satisfaction always leads to improved task performance. Another assumption of content theory is that individuals seek to satisfy all their needs.

Process Theories

Process theory is more 'alive', it is a much more active approach and provides better guidance to managers on motivation techniques. Process theories, then, offer a more dynamic approach. As the name implies the process element relates to the idea of the process of developing motives and is not a static analysis of needs. Process theory argues that being appointed the right task determines human satisfaction. Other assumptions are that it focuses on choice behaviours.

One of the most important process theories is the valency–instrumentality–expectancy theory (VIE) of Vroom (1964). This process theory is normally known as Expectancy Theory:

- *Valency* is the value or anticipated satisfaction from an outcome.
- *Instrumentality* can be interpreted as meaning that if we do one thing we believe it will lead to another.
- *Expectancy* is the probability that action or effort will lead to an outcome (this theory is also known as path – goal theory).

Basically, what this means is that the strength of expectation is based on past experiences, but where past experience is an inadequate guide then motivation may be reduced. Motivation is only likely when a clearly perceived relationship exists between the performance and the outcome. The outcome is seen as a means of satisfying needs. An example of this could be that of a bonus scheme. It only works if the link between effort and reward is clear and the value of the reward is worth the effort.

We can also think of the concept as relating to training. Some might decide to train as accountants because they perceive accountants as professionals who earn good money and have good jobs. Students decide that the effort of studying, perhaps while working, is worth doing for the rewards to be achieved at the end, when they qualify.

If we take this accountancy example one step further we can see that in the past accountancy has been a good profession (indeed middle-class mothers have been telling their children over the years to become doctors, solicitors or accountants). However even accountants have lost their jobs in times of recession. It would be interesting to know whether, because of this, potential accountants are not considering the profession because they perceive that the rewards available for the effort have reduced?

This whole argument leads us into a rather large aside – the issue of the attitudes individuals bring to work. A theory to look at here is the idea of 'orientations to work' put forward by Goldthorpe in his book *The Affluent Worker* (1968).

Goldthorpe looked at the orientation to work of employees and defined this as meaning employees' preferences about rewards for work. Goldthorpe's work identified an *instrumental orientation* to work amongst highly paid manual workers. For these people work is a means to an end, a way of maintaining an affluent lifestyle. The work process can be seen in scientific management terms as an exchange of effort for wages. A further orientation that has been identified is that of *cosmopolitans*, that is people see themselves more as members of a profession than as members of specific organisations. Work may be the central interest in their lives but their focus is broader. Interestingly enough this is one of the biggest differences between Western work practices and Japanese practices. In Japanese culture, once you are employed by a company you are an employee of that company and as such you do whatever job the company wants you to do. The British and Western approach is based more on learning skills that can be transferred across companies.

Getting back to process theories, one of the most significant and useful approaches is that of Porter and Lawler (1968). They described the process model of expectancy theory. This approach goes beyond motivational factors and considers performance as a whole. Motivation, satisfaction and performance are considered as separate variables. Therefore satisfaction is an effect rather than a cause of performance, and performance leads to job satisfaction.

This approach offers managers a tool for identifying the sources of problems concerned with motivation. The model shows the complexity of an individual's motivation patterns. The manager needs to analyse the performance and job satisfaction of subordinates and, in particular,

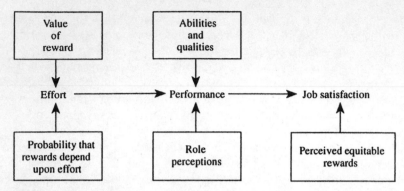

Key:
   Value of rewards is the value to the individual of satisfying needs of security, social esteem, autonomy, self-actualisation.
   Probability that rewards depend upon effort is as perceived by individuals. Their expectations about the relationship between effort and reward.
   Ability: individual characteristics such as intelligence, manual skills, know-how.
   Role Perceptions are what individuals want to do or think they are expected to do. These are positive if the organisation and an individual correspond. They are negative if the organisation and the individuals views do not coincide.

Figure 2.2   Porter and Lawler's process model of motivation

the personal values they attach to rewards, and consider their perception of the likelihood of that reward being met (Figure 2.2).
   So what are some of the other ways of getting individuals to do what the manager or the organisation wants? The next section will look at the effects of power and obedience.

POWER AND OBEDIENCE

Leaders can arise in a number of ways – they may be imposed, appointed, elected or emerge naturally. Leadership implies power, so it is necessary to examine the concept and role of power.

Power

Power can be defined as the ability to achieve outcomes regardless of authority and responsibility. If we take the example of industrial relations, an unofficial strike leader has no official authority to call a strike, and will not have that right written into a job description. However that individual has the power to call strike action.

So, within an organisation the influence of a leader will be dependent upon power. People allow themselves to be influenced if they believe that the leader has power. French and Raven (1953) have identified five areas where power is reflected in management styles.

- *Reward power:* the ability and resources to reward those who comply, by offering pay, promotion, praise or privileges. This type of power is seen very commonly in organisations. Indeed pay, promotion and praise are clearly the responsibility of managers. There is perhaps a suggestion that reward power is a little negative, to be used by managers who cannot get results any other way.
- *Coercive power:* the ability to mete out negative consequences, or remove positive ones. This is the opposite to reward power and works through fear and punishment. This is the style of some managements and perhaps the last resort of some managers. As a source of power it is not going to get the best out of power. Perhaps we can say that many organisations adopt a coercive style with human resources during recession. Employees fear losing their jobs, and management could exploit this by reducing benefits or by making references to promotion being based upon people working hard and doing overtime.
- *Legitimate power:* the leaders' position in the hierarchy will determine the amount of power they have. This type of power is more common in traditional organisations or role culture organisations, where everyone has their place and it is very clear what that place is. This will be determined by size of office, type of car and seniority of personal secretary.
- *Referent power:* people will be influenced by the leader because they respect and admire that person. The leader may have 'charisma'. Some people clearly have charisma and can get others to do what they want. This leader does not have to hold a high position in the hierarchy.
- *Expert power:* others will be influenced by the leader because they believe the leader has superior expertise in a particular area. Every office has a computer expert who is not from the official computer department but who has expertise, can explain things and sort them out.

Obedience

Another area to consider when we think about leadership is that of obedience. Obedience is expected of people by those in positions of authority.

Stanley Milgram (1963) conducted experiments on destructive obedience in the 1960s involving electric shocks being administered. The people administering the shocks were being observed. The victims, who received the shocks (and it should be made clear that the electric shocks were simulated by this group), were part of the experiment. The subjects understood they were participating in an experiment on the effects of punishment on learning. When the victim gave a wrong answer the subject would be required to administer a shock. Also in the room was an experimenter who would give one of four answers when questioned:

1. Please continue or please go on.
2. The experiment requires that you continue.
3. It is absolutely essential that you continue.
4. You have no other choice: you must go on.

The results of the experiment showed that 40 subjects administered shocks and 26 reached the maximum amount of 450 volts, which would mean causing severe pain. The subjects were all under stress and one observer is quoted as saying:

> I observed a mature and initially poised businessman enter the laboratory smiling and confident. Within twenty minutes, he was reduced to a twitching, stuttering wreck who was rapidly approaching a point of nervous collapse. He constantly pulled on his earlobe and twisted his hands. At one point he pushed his fist into his forehead and muttered 'Oh God. Let's stop it!' And yet he continued to respond to every word of the experimenter and obeyed to the end (Milgram, 1963).

Milgram was criticised with regard to ethics, but the results showed he induced a high level of obedience from people who otherwise considered their actions to be wrong. It is not unusual for individuals to do things in the organisation or in groups that they would not do otherwise.

GROUPS AND TEAMS

At what point does a collection of individuals become a team or a group? Some of the conditions that apply are that there should be communication, probably face-to-face, and the objectives of the members should be similar. Often there is an external threat that brings the group together. Group can be defined as primary, secondary, interest and peer.

- *Primary:* these groups are formed by people who freely choose to mix together. An example might be two or three people who regularly go swimming together. There is nothing formal in the arrangement.
- *Secondary:* these groups start to develop a structure and objectives. So our swimmers might recruit more people and form a club with a president, treasurer and other elected officials.
- *Interest:* an interest group is one where individuals come together for social or economic interests. A good example might be an Institute of Personnel and Development (IPD) branch meeting. Some people come for either objective and some for both.
- *Peer:* peer groups are made up of people of the same or similar ages who share the similar cultural values and interests. An example could be a Rugby Club where the members enjoy playing rugby, and drinking beer!

The Formation of Groups

The most important work in this area is that of Tuckman (1965), who proposes some stages that groups go through:

- *Forming*: members begin to see themselves and others as having common interests.
- *Storming*: at this point the group starts to set its own norms and ground rules. Also, different roles start to emerge.
- *Norming*: the behaviour of the group starts to be more predictable as common norms of behaviour within the group start to be established.
- *Performing*: according to Tuckman a mature team can then start to perform. The rate at which different groups reach this point can vary considerably.

A fifth level is often added to this model – *mourning*. It can be very traumatic when close teams break up and the emotions generated need to be managed very carefully.

This process reflects quite well what actually goes on. If you think of times when you have joined a team, there is great pressure to conform to the existing norms of the group. From the other side, if you are a member of an existing team and a new member arrives it can certainly affect the dynamics and cause a state of flux for a while. What happens is that the group and the new member will both adjust their norms. So the group may move slightly to accommodate the new person.

One of the ideas floated in the previous section is that different team members play different parts. Effective teams need to have a range of roles. If all the team members pay great attention to detail there will be no one to plan or look at the longer term. Some organisations take this idea very seriously and may identify the predominant styles of existing team members when recruiting so that they choose a person who will complement the team. Alternatively existing teams can examine their preferred styles and see the gaps (if any exist) and allocate work accordingly.

The basic idea is that if you take a group of people with have diverse abilities, interests and experiences then the synergy, or sum of this diversity will be greater than that which they could achieve as individuals.

Perhaps the best known writer in this area is Dr Meredith Belbin. Belbin (1981) has devised a questionnaire to indicate preferred styles. Belbin proposes eight main roles that people adopt and that teams need in order to be effective. An individual may have one clear preferred role or two or three that are similar in strength. These roles are:

- *Chair:* someone who controls the way the team goes about achieving its goals; this will be by effectively using the resources and potential of all the team members.
- *Company worker:* a person who is good at carrying out plans systematically and efficiently, turning concepts and plans into practical working procedures.
- *Completer–finisher:* this person pays great attention to detail, actively looks for work that requires great attention and enjoys doing it (without being disturbed!).
- *Monitor–evaluator:* this person is good at analysing problems, and is also good at monitoring what the team should be doing.
- *Plant:* this is the role of the person who has ideas and probably looks at the overall picture at the strategic level.

- *Resource investigator*: this person will create external links and may subsequently negotiate with other teams. Such a person will also be good at exploring ideas and opportunities. We could probably say that he or she is more outward facing.
- *Shaper*: this role involves shaping the way the team works. A shaper will be concerned with the objectives of the whole team and shaping group discussions.
- *Team worker*: this role involves supporting the other members of the team. A team worker will be good at improving communication and fostering team spirit.

The role(s) that an individual shows preferences for are to be taken in the context of a team. The scores in isolation may not mean so much. However my own roles (when I was in a team) reveal me to be a resource investigator and a team worker. I believe that the roles identified still have substance in explaining the work I do now. The resource investigator part is quite useful now as I run my own business and look for ways to make my living. My team worker needs are met by associations with clients. For the educational establishments for whom I do some work, I am able to pop in for a chat and even attend social events. For other clients it is important for me to feel that I am working with them, as part of a team, to help them solve their problems.

Effective versus Ineffective Groups

It is useful to compare some of the characteristics of both effective and ineffective teams against certain criteria.

- *Objectives*: for the effective group the objectives will be very clear. In the ineffective group there will be uncertainty and a lack of clarity about what the group task is.
- *Communication*: in the effective group there will be a lot of discussion, with everyone participating. In ineffective groups there may be a lot of discussion but not everyone will be involved and it certainly will not be directed.
- *Decision making*: in effective teams, decisions will be made after discussion and will be based on consensus. In ineffective teams decisions may not be made after consultation, indeed decisions may be made prematurely.

- *Leadership style*: effective leaders will coach the group and provide guidance. Ineffective team leaders are those that are autocratic, defensive or secretive.
- *Self-evaluation*: effective teams will spend time reviewing their own performance, looking for improvements. Ineffective teams do not examine their own processes and do not self-evaluate.

INTER-GROUP CONFLICT

Conflict is an inevitable part of groups. If we look at it in terms of how effective and ineffective teams will cope with conflict, as in the analysis above, the effective group will handle any conflict in the open and will be prepared to confront conflict issues. With ineffective teams conflicts may fester and result in open or guerilla warfare.

Conflict can arise for a variety of reasons, such as personality, individual differences and the environment. One view proposed by Makin, Cooper and Cox (1991) is that, as individuals, we want to promote a positive self-image. To support this we join groups that will help us to achieve it. Perhaps this explains why people are prepared to pay very large sums of money to join certain exclusive golf clubs. Makin *et al.* propose that people are prepared to go to great lengths to discriminate in favour of their own team, and therefore enhance their own prestige. The evidence of this is seen in organisations where there is withholding of information between groups or even deliberate misinformation.

Another explanation for conflict is competition. There may be competition for scarce resources. When interactions do take place group members are likely to spend more time attending to their own spokesperson's performance than to what the other group says.

Makin, Cooper and Cox (1991) propose areas that have to be addressed to manage conflict effectively:

- *Trust*: trust takes a long time to develop but can be quickly destroyed. Trust is an indication of openness between group members.
- *Communication*: improving communication between groups can help to reduce conflict. Unfortunately it can also make the situation worse.

● *Domination*: power can be used to resolve differences, although the group with the most power may dominate the weaker groups.

Conflict, then, is almost inevitable, indeed some competition is desirable. In organisations managers under pressure may be tempted to concentrate on short-term goals and therefore use domination or power to achieve their ends. Managers need to achieve a balance between the benefits and dangers of intergroup rivalry in their particular circumstances.

Part II
Organisational Necessities

3 Compensation and Benefit Systems

Organisations have to compensate their staff for using their time and expertise for the furtherance of the organisations' objectives. Paying for effort, or performance is the Nirvana that many managers have searched for. Managers are required to distinguish the exceptional contributors from the ordinary and find out what it is that motivates them to produce exceptional effort or performance, and then to reproduce it.

Organisations need to manage reward. That means designing and maintaining a reward system that leads to the improvement of organisational performance. A reward system cannot easily stand in isolation so information and analysis of market rates and values has to be sought. To ensure that internal differentials are maintained and to make external comparison meaningful, organisations establish job evaluation systems. These systems are based on analysis of job design and the creation of job descriptions. To maintain a reward system grading structures and job ranges need to be established. Types of payment must be considered, such as incentives for sales staff or factory operatives, and profit sharing or merit payments for managers. Fringe benefits can be used to make up a 'total remuneration package'. Other benefits may be compulsory by law, such as sick pay arrangements or maternity benefits. The distribution of reward may also be subject to union participation or agreement.

The most successful compensation systems will be those that are considered by the staff who operate under them to be fair and equitable. If the recipients of the system feel that they and their colleagues have been rewarded appropriately, relative to the marketplace and effort, then effective human resource management has taken place.

Reward management concentrates on the retention element of human resource management, a definition of which is to recruit, retain, motivate, and develop staff.

An example of how important compensation and benefits is to organisations can be shown by some recent information from the Metropolitan Police. Of their annual budget of £1.6 billion, wages came to 87 per cent of the total.

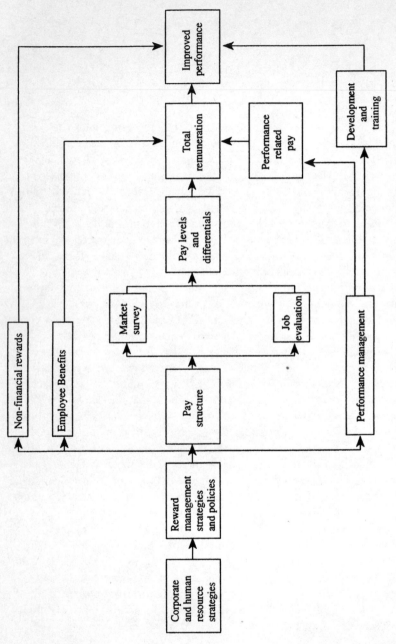

Figure 3.1   Armstrong's model of reward management strategy and processes

CORPORATE AND HUMAN RESOURCE STRATEGIES

Reward management, if used properly, assists the organisation to achieve its objectives of obtaining and retaining the staff it requires and increasing their motivation and commitment.

Reward systems can also be used in other ways. During the recession in the UK in the 1990s companies have tried to reduce overheads and have therefore only given salary reviews or bonuses to certain key staff in the knowledge that other employees will become dissatisfied and take their labour elsewhere. The organisation has achieved its objective of reducing overheads by managing the reward system, by rewarding people according to their actual or perceived value to the organisation. The system also recognises that staff as individuals have different needs and can be incentivised in different ways. For example in the UK the company car is often a perquisite that reflects status. Junior or middle managers can often be offered a car instead of a salary increase when the value of the car to the company (when it has depreciated over four or five years, for accounting purposes) might actually be less than the value of an increase in basic salary.

Armstrong (1991) proposes a model of reward management strategy and processes (Figure 3.1).

REWARD MANAGEMENT STRATEGIES AND POLICIES

Non-Financial Rewards

Motivation has already been looked at in the previous chapter but it is useful to look at theories of money and motivation:

- *Economic man*: F.W. Taylor (1947) and the scientific management school proposed that the best way to improve performance was to provide direct financial rewards. In effect payment by results.
- *Human relations theory*: Elton Mayo's conclusions for the Hawthorne experiments (Roethlisberger and Dickson, 1939) proposed that it is the intrinsic factors of recognition and fulfilment that lead to greater productivity. Indeed one survey of 42 000 people put pay as the sixth most important motivating factor.

- *Contingency theory*: the contingency approach is a link between the economic and human relations theories and it proposes that there is no one best way to motivate individuals.

What is clear then is that money is not the only factor in motivation. Achievement, challenge, recognition and security are all important. The major motivator at any one time is determined by individuals' attitudes and preferences.

Perhaps the importance of pay is not that you have enough, but what you have relative to what others have. People inevitably compare themselves to their peers and managers and if they feel that others are getting more reward or appreciation for what is perceived as less effort they become dissatisfied (see the two-factor theory of Hertzberg in Chapter 2).

Employee Benefits

Employee benefits can be offered in addition to pay. Some of the reasons why organisations offer these benefits are:

- As a method of rewarding employees and offering them benefits in a tax efficient manner.
- To demonstrate to employees that the company cares for them.
- To retain employees, often by 'tying' them into, for example, share option schemes, which are exempt of tax if the shares are kept in the scheme for five years.
- The benefits are industry norms, for example, mortgage subsidies are offered by the big UK clearing banks.
- The organisation may be able to negotiate arrangements or discounts that the individual cannot.

Actual benefits may apply under several of the headings above. For example a benefit introduced because it is prevalent amongst industry sector competitors may be sold to staff as an example of a caring employer. Also employers and employees may see benefits from different perspectives. The 50-year-old directors of an organisation may have established an excellent pension scheme. This employee benefit, devised to attract and retain staff, may not have the same significance to a 19-year-old office junior.

Other benefits may be in place due to legislation pertaining in the country of origin. In the European Union member states have to offer maternity provisions. In the UK there is a minimum standard set by legislation. Individual companies are able to offer enhanced conditions to the minimum requirement.

The types of benefit most regularly offered can include:

- Basic pay, guaranteed by a contract of employment.
- Sick pay: companies may have a statutory obligation to provide sick pay. Provision of sick pay is normally related to length of service. Some organisations offer regular medical screening for more senior staff or older employees. In the UK some organisations are offering 'well-women' checks for female staff.
- Private health insurance: organisations can insure staff under PHI schemes so that if employees are forced to give up work due to injuries sustained at or resulting from their work they will have a guaranteed income up to retirement age.
- Pensions: most UK employers offer employees the opportunity to join an occupational pension scheme, whether contributory or non-contributory. Pensions are usually regarded as the most important employee benefit. Members of a scheme build up the right to guaranteed income for themselves or their dependents upon retirement or death. In countries such as the UK, where there is a state earnings-related pension scheme, occupational or company pension schemes offer employees the chance to enhance this minimum entitlement. Pensions can also fulfil higher level esteem needs, as in the case of senior managers, who are often offered enhanced schemes.
- Private medical insurance: in the UK there is a state funded national health service but some employers offer membership of a private health scheme to employees. The organisation gains in that employees can be guaranteed immediate access to specialists for non-urgent consultations and treatment. The organisation is also seen to be caring for its employees.
- Holidays: national legislation may determine basic holiday entitlement or there may be regional or industry averages. It is usual for the amount of holiday entitlement to increase with seniority and service. In the UK the average is between 20 days and 30 days per year. In the US the average is 10 to 15 days.
- Other absence entitlement: many European companies now offer other benefits, such as paternity leave for varying periods. It is also usual to be granted paid leave when sitting professional examinations.
- Financial benefits: some organisations, particularly finance-related ones, offer benefits to employees in the form of loans at preferential

rates, mortgages, relocation assistance and interest free season ticket loans.

- Sports and social: many organisations run or subsidise sports and social clubs. Organisations can use their size and buying power to negotiate reduced club membership fees.

- Company cars: the provision of company cars to non-essential users in the UK is an example of esteem benefits. The provision of a car is a sign of status internally to the organisation and externally to society. Car schemes usually have very carefully controlled levels relating to status in the organisation. An example is of a company in the financial services sector with 330 employees, of which 100 are company car drivers (perhaps one quarter of these may be job-related cars for sales people). In total 30 per cent of employees have company cars. An example of car grades comes from another financial sector company in London:

Level	Value (£)	Staff level
One	22 000	Directors
Two	17 500	Subsidiary directors/senior managers
Three	15 000	Middle managers
Four	11 000	Junior managers

- Training: Ford UK operates a policy that allows all employees a number of days training per year. Employees are allowed to use some of the time to attend courses on matters totally unrelated to their particular job. The company is attempting to improve personal satisfaction, achieve development and therefore improve overall performance.

Pay Structures

A pay structure needs to be appropriate to the needs of the organisation, that is it needs to be flexible enough to incorporate the type and level of employee to be covered. The structure must be able to reflect the external market in relation to supply and demand. There must be scope to reward high performance and achievement. Employees need to see that the system is consistent and fair and that it provides a basis for career planning. Structures that reflect all these requirements are known as 'ladder' or 'step' systems. They define:

- Job or generic categories.
- Salary (and/or grade).
- The size of the band.

An example of a pay structure from a company in the UK is as follows:

Grade	Support staff	Coordinator	Assistant manager/ Team leader	Manager	Senior manager
11					———
10					Group
9				———	V
8				Group	———
7			———	IV	
6			Group	———	
5		———	III		
4		Group	———		
3	———	II			
2	Group	———			
1	I				
	———				

Generic job groupings

This approach places an individual in a grouping with similar staff. Position in the group is determined by ability. There is some overlap between the groups so that an experienced high performing team leader can be earning more than an inexperienced manager. Each group will have its own set of benefits, for example:

	Holidays	Car band	Share option scheme	Paid overtime	Salary Min.	Max.
Group V: Senior manager	30	1	Yes	No	30 900	75 000
Group IV: Manager	25	2	No	No	21 300	41 700
Group III: Asst. manager/ Team leader	25	3	No	No	15 000	28 700
Group II: Coordinator	20	N/A	No	Yes	11 000	20 900
Group I: Support staff	20	N/A	No	Yes	9100	17 600

Other forms of pay structure are as follows.

Piecework

Payment is on the production of finished items – no need for close supervision and the work can be completed by homeworkers. This payment system was pioneered by Taylor (1947) and its legacy is still with us:

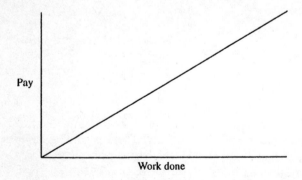

Flat rate

Payment remains constant irrespective of rate:

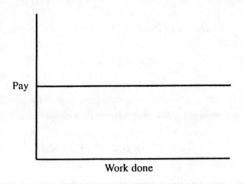

Piecework and flat rate

This system operates where pay is related to work done (up to a preset limit), but work done after that target has been achieved is on a flat rate:

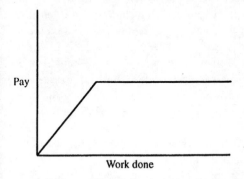

Once a pay structure has been created the next s' external environment for market values and rat' internal relativities through job evaluation.

Analysis of Market Rates and Values

To a large extent market forces are the key indicator in fixing the rate for a job. Certainly the external market needs to be regularly and systematically checked. The information obtained should always be treated warily. There will always be different rates paid by different companies for the same job. External market information therefore gives indicators of possible rates. Armstrong (1991) proposes four key sources from which that information can be obtained:

- *Company surveys*: companies can either organise surveys themselves or use consultants to conduct a survey of similar companies. These surveys are aimed at similar jobs in similar companies. There may already be an informal exchange of information between these comparable companies. The results of the survey can be offered in an anonymous summary to participating companies (hence the fact that these surveys are normally carried out by consultants). These company surveys often concentrate on one particular area, such as provision of company cars or a comparison of, say, all the sales jobs. Company surveys can often lead to formal club surveys.
- *Club surveys*: salary clubs have been operating successfully for many years. Companies in a single industry club together and each contribute to and pay for a survey over a number of years. By majority vote companies can be asked to leave or be offered an opportunity to join. When a survey has been running for a number of years it is possible for the managers responsible to develop a good understanding of the jobs in the survey and what any changes indicate. A good example of where a club survey is of benefit is in relation to graduates. All the survey members will be aware of a range for the industry or sector for what is a notoriously difficult position to place. The oil companies have a very well known and comprehensive survey that has been running for many years.
- *General published surveys*: these are surveys that are produced by consultancies and cover large bandings, such as financial services or retail. They are the accumulated knowledge of the consultancies. They are available for purchase and may even reflect geographical locations.
  Analysis of job advertisements: a relatively cheap and simple way to gain market information is to search relevant papers and journals

for jobs that fit the same description. This kind of survey is often used to assess whether there is a problem or not – and whether further detailed analysis is required. It should also be remembered that the salaries and benefits offered are likely to be maximum rates or top-of-the-range and may not reflect the salary and benefits actually offered.

The information gleaned still has to be interpreted and related back to the organisation. The organisation has to decide whether it wants to accept the rates and if so where it wants to place itself. Some companies boast that they are 'upper quartile' and therefore their mid-point needs to be above the median.

Matching all the benefits offered by competitors can be costly, but it can be even more costly not to!

Job Evaluation

Job evaluation may be described, in broad terms, as a process used at company – but sometimes at industry – level in order to determine the relationship between jobs and to establish a systematic structure of wage rates for them (Trades Union Congress, 1964).

Job evaluation aims to establish a rank order of jobs, measure the differences between jobs and group them appropriately. Job evaluation also aims to ensure objective judgement and promote a systematic process (for assessing the value of jobs) that is equitable. The different techniques of job evaluation all have the same overriding criteria:

● Job evaluation is concerned with assessing the job and not the performance of the job holder.
● Job evaluation needs to be conducted by experienced practitioners in a systematic way.
● Job evaluation produces a structure against which a salary structure must be put, relative to the needs of the organisation.

Job evaluation schemes can be non-quantitative or quantitative:

● Non-quantitative
  – ranking
  – job classification

- Quantitative
  - factor comparison
  - points rating

Ranking

This process involves comparing jobs and arranging them in order of importance, difficulty and/or value to the company. The question to be asked is: what is the importance of the job to end results? Ranking schemes operate by identifying key jobs in the organisation, for example the most important and the least important jobs, and then ranking all jobs within that framework. Normally benchmark jobs are decided at key points of the hierarchy and jobs positioned around them. These schemes are often found to be easy to operate at the extremes but fitting in mid-range jobs can be problematic. There is also a tendency to assess how the job holder is carrying out the job and not the job itself.

Job classification

This system is based on initial definition of a grading structure. That is, the number and characteristics of the grade are decided and jobs are placed in the grades accordingly. The typical 'discernible differences' used to differentiate the groups would be factors such as skill, responsibility, complexity, decision making, knowledge or education and training required. Typically general descriptions will be written for comparison against real jobs.

These two systems are relatively simple and inexpensive. Organisations often have to create a large number of descriptions to accommodate jobs that have characteristics that overlap those of other jobs.

Factor comparison

Factor comparison consists of ranking different positions against a series of factors and not against a whole job. Therefore a series of factors are agreed upon, such as:

- Minimum education
- Decision making
- Supervisory responsibility

- Specialist skills
- Training

Jobs are placed in rank order against the criteria (each criterion has a scale of 1 to 5), so that a cumulative score is achieved for each job. Factor comparison systems are useful for clerical and administrative positions but are perhaps not sophisticated enough to cope with specialist or senior management positions, where measuring degrees of problem solving is required.

Points rating

Points rating job evaluation systems are the most widely used. They require an analysis of factors common to all jobs. The amount of factors present indicates level in the hierarchy. The factors that are commonly used are skill, responsibility, complexity, decisions and contact with others.

The best known points rating system is that of Hay Management Consultants. The scheme was developed in the 1940s by Ned Hay, who identified nine factors common to all jobs:

Hay proposed that levels 1, 2 and 5 are the key indicators for senior jobs in the organisation and levels 3, 4 and 5 will be the key levels for the remaining jobs. Jobs are evaluated against three key characteristics:

- Know-how
- Problem solving
- Accountability

The position of the job against these criteria indicates a certain number of points. Basically the greater the number of points accrued the more important the job.

These schemes require that thought and effort goes into the job assessment process. There is an appearance of objectivity although clearly they are highly subjective. The disadvantages are that systematic evaluation of all (or benchmark) jobs is costly, time consuming and complex. Skilled practitioners of a points rating scheme can make jobs appear greater than they are, in comparison with other jobs in the organisation. Lastly a fault of points rating systems is that jobs are assessed in 'batch' and are not 'real time' – the assessment is only correct at that moment in time – and they are not dynamic in the way that the real jobs of the organisation are.

Equal value

In the UK, under amendments to the Equal Pay Act of 1984, job evaluation has taken an extra significance in the workplace. The Equal Pay legislation can be used to support sex discrimination cases. Any woman can claim equal pay with any man (or vice versa) if she believes that her work is equally demanding under such factors as effort, skill and decision making. A study should be undertaken to evaluate jobs against those terms.

The first case brought was *Haywood v. Cammell Laird Shipbuilders*, where a cook's work was found to be equal to that of a printer, a carpenter and a thermal insulation engineer. A more recent case in 1990 resulted in substantial pay increases being awarded to check-out operators in supermarkets. An extensive job evaluation review found that check-out work, mainly conducted by women, was equal to the job of storeman, mainly held by men.

Pay Levels and Differentials

The decision taken on pay structure provides a framework for the input of information on market rates and values and internal job evaluation.

The result is a structure of pay levels, including differentials, that meet the needs of the organisation as it attempts to:

- Attract
- Retain
- Motivate
- Develop

Performance Management

The last of the four key areas that Armstrong (1991) proposes in his model of reward management is the area of performance management. Performance management, or profit related pay, is an element of compensation that is more closely linked to motivation. That is, individual, team or company performance will have a direct impact on salary. So, for example, in some sectors such as life assurance sales salespeople do not receive a basic salary, rather earnings are relative to the number and value of policies sold. Other sectors, such as local government, have traditionally had no mechanism to reward performance other than basic salary.

In this section five different methods of reward management will be explored.

- Individual performance schemes
- Team performance schemes
- Profit sharing
- Executive performance schemes
- Incentives for sales staff

Individual performance schemes

Individual schemes are in addition to basic pay. Often they are linked to a reward-based appraisal scheme. In these schemes the level of performance attained by the individual equates to a fixed figure for all staff in that grade or department. That is, exceptional performance generates a 10 per cent bonus or salary increase. Those who have not performed so well will get a smaller percentage bonus or increase, and so on.

Companies favour offering bonuses as incentives as they tend to be used to purchase exceptional items. Alternatively they are given at a certain time of the year, such as in advance of the summer holidays, at Christmas or at the end of the year.

Individual performance can be closely targeted to match the broader organisational objectives, but it may come at the expense of teamwork. Another problem is that subjectivity in assessment is ever present and assessors may be unwilling to 'mark down' a poor performance as it is easier to give a small increase than none.

Team performance schemes

Team or group schemes can be usefully targeted for work teams. They make no allowance for individual performance but are in effect rewarding individuals who can work well together. These schemes may also encourage competition between groups, which may be counterproductive. Also specialists or technical staff may not fit easily in to a team and share team goals. This approach is particularly relevant to 'empowered' organisations (see Chapter 11).

Profit sharing

Profit sharing is usually offered to the whole company and is very clearly related to profits. It can be difficult for individuals to relate how their individual performance affects company profits. Also profit sharing is often presented as a percentage of basic salary. This practice can often be counter productive as it demotivates the majority of staff whose payment is relatively small, due to their salary being low, and does not increase the motivation of highly paid staff. One alternative practised in some firms in London is to set aside a percentage of profits and divide it equally among all staff.

Under current UK law an Inland Revenue registered profit related pay scheme is in operation. The key features of this scheme are:

- A percentage is set aside for sharing when a company achieves a pre-agreed profit level.
- The larger the profit the more there is in the pool.
- The pool figure is divided by total salaries over the period in question.
- A monetary sum is arrived at that is then multiplied by each individual salary to distribute the pool.

Executive performance schemes

Executive performance schemes can be related to achieving financial targets and can be a higher percentage than the performance pay received by other managers. Often executive incentives can involve share allocation. Offering bonuses as a share option that can only be cashed in after three or four years is common. Share option schemes are a useful method of tying senior managers to the organisation. The problem with this approach is that it is then very difficult (or expensive) to remove them again. It can also result in senior managers being very supportive of the status quo as they do not want to take any risks with the investment they have in the organisation.

Incentives for sales staff

Sales staff often have very complicated salary structures; structures that are designed to incentivise and motivate them towards achieving the targets required by the sales operation. Organisations go to great lengths, as they perceive the sales person who is bringing in new business is the most important person in the organisation. More modern ideas of management appreciate that the internal customer can be just as important as the external customer. The fact that organisations can create well-targeted sales pay structures means that they should be achievable for all staff.

An example of a simple incentive would be of a salesperson who is selling two products – computers at £1 000 and photocopiers at £500. The company makes a profit of £100 on computers and £50 on photocopiers. In the marketplace photocopiers are easier to sell than computers but the company wants sales to comprise 75 per cent computers and 25 per cent photocopiers. The company incentivises the salesperson by offering a commission of £10 per computer and £4 per photocopier, with a bonus of £1000 if a 75:25 per cent mix is achieved every quarter. In this scenario it is clear to the salesperson what the company wants achieved.

More sophisticated schemes could involve offering salespeople 1 per cent of the generated business if they achieve above a certain amount, say £10 000, and then offering a further 0.5 per cent of anything above £100 000.

Incentives for sales staff, then, should be treated differently from other categories of employee.

Development and Training

Training has a key part to play in reward management. It can be, and often is, offered as a reward but its greater use is as a means of achieving a better performance and therefore greater reward.

Coaching and training assistance can be available to staff who want to achieve higher levels of performance in their own job or want to learn the skills and techniques of another. Many companies in the UK operate graduate training schemes where it is very clear what the minimum training requirement is to be eligible. Other jobs in the organisation may also have clear requirements. For example it is unlikely that the finance director is not a qualified or chartered accountant. In the UK the market for accountants in the boom years of the late 1980s was such that qualification would immediately result in a 10–30 per cent increase as newly qualified accountants were in great demand but very short in supply.

Total Remuneration

All the elements discussed in this chapter contribute to the total remuneration package. A typical package offered to a middle manager in a London company could consist of the following:

- Basic salary
- Company profit sharing scheme (up to 10 per cent of basic salary)
- Share purchase scheme
- Medical insurance
- Non-contributory pension scheme
- Company car (plus free petrol)
- Interest-free season ticket loan
- Holiday
- Life assurance

A recent approach to the management of total remuneration is the introduction of 'cafeteria benefits', or flexible remuneration systems. Woodley (1990) proposes that the basic premise is that 'individual choice is seen as a benefit in its own right'.

The simplest way of offering significant individual choice is to take four or five key benefits such as pension, life assurance, car and holidays and offer three bands of choice. Individuals can then move up or down to get the package that suits them best. Normally points are allocated for the benefits and individuals can choose, say, 10 points spread across certain benefits. They may choose a better car but no medical insurance.

A cafeteria approach may be suitable for attracting women returners or it may offer a competitive edge in the labour market. An effective remuneration package will attract, retain and motivate staff.

There are good examples of these schemes. The first is by Lowe (1992) of the retailer Burtons. Lowe proposes that cafeteria systems or 'pick and mix' schemes originated in the US, where staff health insurance is very expensive and companies are very keen to wean staff off them. The Burton scheme was introduced to an initial group of 1200 managers and provided core benefits and flexible benefits, the main core benefit being a pension. Burtons felt that the new system would enhance staff relations and benefit the recruitment and selection process.

A second recent example was quoted in *Personnel Management* in April 1994. Mercury communications are introducing a scheme for all employees. The items available are pensions, annual leave, life cover, cars, healthcare and dental insurance. Several of the benefits are more closely controlled. So pension options mean that employees can enhance the existing scheme but they can not reduce their contribution.

Improved Performance

The Armstrong model of reward management has as its last box 'improved performance'. Clearly all the elements must pull together to motivate and direct staff along the right lines for the organisation to achieve a sustainable competitive advantage. A key component of this will be to communicate to staff how the whole system works and how it will benefit them.

4 Recruitment and Selection

If people are the most important asset of the organisation the practices adopted need to be of value to an organisation in achieving its aims. A particularly important area is that of recruitment and selection. For recruitment and selection to achieve this it needs to:

● Reflect the culture and values of the organisation.
● Involve line management.
● Be good practice.

REFLECTING THE CULTURE AND VALUES OF THE ORGANISATION

The values and beliefs that go towards forming the culture need to be reflected in the way the recruitment system works. So, for example, whether companies reply quickly and politely to all applications submitted says something about the company to the applicant. The style of advertising also gives messages about the organisation; historically clearing banks in the UK have used 'traditional' advertisements that rely on large amounts of copy but no visuals. In comparison computer companies tend to use full colour, exciting visuals but little copy in their advertisements.

Successful companies can develop a recruitment philosophy; in effect a mission statement for their recruitment. Often companies will develop a logo or catchphrase to use in all their advertising. Current examples are:

● NAAFI: Serving the Services.
● National and Provincial Building Society: Make a Bee-line for N & P.
● Greater Glasgow Health Board: Our Business is Health.
● ICI: World Class.
● Lloyds Bowmaker: Investing in People for the Future.

Recruitment decisions could be for life so it is essential that companies seeking to retain and develop their workforce should ensure they have recruited the right people. The recruitment process is very visible. It provides a way for external people to be able to make assessments about the company. People applying to FTSE 100 companies expect to be treated in a professional manner by the company. Recruitment and selection is not a PR exercise but the effect it has on public relations should be considered.

INVOLVING LINE MANAGEMENT

It is important that line managers feel part of the selection process and 'own' the selection decisions – the new recruit is going to work for them and not the personnel department. The recruiting manager needs to feel confident that the prospective employee will be able to do the work required. Personnel can establish recruitment procedures or systems to assist line managers and provide advice on appropriate selection methods. Personnel can have input into the recruitment decision, but usually it is not the casting vote. Personnel can provide training and guidance to line managers on the techniques, legal requirements and good practice of selection.

GOOD PRACTICE

A good recruitment system needs to have three elements. It needs to be:

- *Effective*: are you recruiting the best candidates? This may be measured by looking at company performance.
- *Efficient*: are there established procedures? Are new recruits joining the company in a cost-effective way.
- *Fair*: do you recruit in a non-discriminatory way? (Even in countries where equal opportunities are not enforced by law the objectives should be the same, that is, are we attracting and recruiting the best candidates?)

To achieve this the recruitment system needs to be well structured, systematic and formalised.

These questions, and others, will be addressed in the next section, which will follow through the processes of a typical recruitment procedure, exploring the alternatives and highlighting good practice.

RECRUITMENT PROCEDURE

The approach outlined is one that would be expected of a Western company where recruitment is *specific* – that is, applicants are sought for a particular position rather – than *general* as occurs in Japan, where recruitment is to provide an 'establishment' and then develop people from the establishment as the company sees fit. Employees of the company do any job that is required of them. The typical stages of a recruitment procedure are:

1. Organisation analysis.
2. Job analysis.
3. Establish job descriptions.
4. Formulate a job specification.
5. Consider any legal requirements.
6. Attract candidates.
7. Advertise.
8. Handle applications.
9. Selection.
   – interviews
   – testing
   – other selection methods.
10. Selection decision making.
11. Monitor the success of the selection process.
12. Induction.

Organisation Analysis

Recruitment may be required either when an existing employee leaves or a new position is created. Whatever the reason, organisation analysis needs to be completed to assess whether there really is a vacancy or whether the work could be done somewhere else. Reorganisation of work or training could solve the problem. Alternatively someone could be promoted into the position as it is probably better for organisations to try to recruit at the bottom of the hierarchy. This approach has two benefits: it is cheaper and it allows the organisation to train and develop staff into the existing culture. Alternatively new positions may be part of a strategic manpower plan and these should be checked to make sure they are still current.

The context of the job should be clarified. Where does it fit into the existing structure relative to grades, pay and reporting lines? Is it clear what the recruitment procedure will be? That is, many companies in the UK promise staff that all vacancies will first be notified internally (usually with a proviso saying 'where appropriate').

One common check on organisational analysis is to have all vacancies 'signed off' by the head of human resources or Chief Executive Officer (CEO), that way they can monitor whether recruitment is in line with the corporate plan.

Job Analysis

This stage in the process is a systematic and detailed analysis of the job. Amongst the more common methods of achieving this are:

- Observing the job: checking that you understand all that the job holder does.
- Interview the job holder.
- Work study techniques: measuring and timing actions (remember scientific management).
- Diary method: job holder completes a diary recording all tasks carried out.
- Work performance: the analyst performs the job.
- Critical incident technique: observing the key incidents in the job, both good and bad.

All these methods are open to some subjectivity but if carried out in a systematic way they will provide useful information.

The method of job analysis will therefore indicate something about the culture of the organisation carrying out the analysis.

Job Descriptions

Job descriptions have many uses in human resource management but in relation to recruitment their purpose is to set the parameters of the job.

A good job description covers the total requirements of the job; the who, what, where, when and why. The key elements will be:

- Organisation chart of where the job fits in.
- A short statement of the main purpose of the job.
- The key responsibilities of the job (usually no more than six).
- How the responsibilities are to be carried out.
- The scope of the job.

Other requirements could include: resources managed, relationships with others, working conditions, training and development requirements.

In recent years there has been a tendency in some organisations to use a 'key results area' approach. Instead of the job description describing duties, tasks or activities it is written in terms of the key results to be achieved by the job holder.

Job Specifications

The job specification is identification of the skills, knowledge and attitudes required to perform the tasks – these are combined with the duties identified in the job description.

The job specification will be influenced by the person specification, which looks at attitudes and personal skills. Careful analysis of the requirements will enable you to establish the parameters of the person required so that you can identify the requirements that are:

- Essential
- Desirable

Perhaps the best known person specification system is Alec Rodger's seven-point plan (1952):

- Physical make-up: health, appearance, bearing, speech.
- Attainments: education, qualifications, experience.
- General intelligence: intellectual capacity.
- Special aptitudes: mechanical, manual dexterity facility in using words and figures.
- Interests: intellectual, practical, constructional, physically active, social, artistic.
- Disposition: acceptability, influence over others, steadiness, dependability, self-reliance.

- Circumstances: any special demands of the job, such as ability to work unsocial hours, travel abroad and so on.

A modified version of Rodger's seven-point plan:

- Physical make-up
- Attainments
- Skills
- Work interests
- Work attitudes
- Personality
- Circumstances

An alternative person specification system is the Munro Fraser (1958) five-fold grading system:

- Impact on others: physical make-up, appearance, speech and manner.
- Acquired qualifications: education, vocational training, work experience.
- Innate attitudes: quickness of comprehension and aptitude for learning.
- Motivation: traditional goals, consistency and determination in following them up.
- Adjustment: emotional stability, ability to stand up to stress and ability to get on with people.

Recently these approaches have been criticised for being inherently discriminatory. Assessing people on criteria such as physical ability may mean that women or disabled people are discriminated against. Surely, in our sophisticated technological age there are aids available to compensate for brute strength.

Later in this chapter there is a section on competency-based recruitment, which perhaps offers a more objective and reliable way of recruiting.

Legal Requirements

Legal requirements in the guise of anti-discrimination legislation is in force in the US and most European countries. In the UK the chief legislation is found in the Sex Discrimination Act, 1975 and the

Race Relations Act, 1976. Both acts recognise three main types of discrimination:

- Direct: treating people less favourably because of their gender or on the grounds of race. Selection for recruitment is quoted as a key area where less favourable treatment may occur.
- Indirect: applying conditions, such as requiring a good standard of written English for a manual labourer's job.
- Victimisation: provides redress for those who feel they have been victimised in their employment because they brought a complaint against their employer.

The implications for recruitment and selection are that effective job analysis will lead to an unbiased job specification against which the best candidate can be recruited. Good practice in recruitment procedures will ensure that other types of discrimination do not arise in areas such as age or disability.

Discrimination is an insidious process; the old adage is that we recruit in our own image and perpetuate the discrimination. I like to listen to *Test Match Special* on the wireless and frequently the commentators, who are all ex-professional cricketers, comment that only other professional cricketers can administer or comment on the game of cricket. I wonder if this is really true.

Attracting Candidates

The best medium is the one that reaches the target group in the most cost-effective way. Some of the most common methods, plus their advantages and disadvantages, are as follows.

- *Internal recruitment*: offers opportunities for the promotion and development of existing staff. It is an open system that gives everyone an opportunity to apply. However it may reinforce the existing composition of the company and therefore not reach other external applicants; what fate befalls staff who apply for internal jobs and do not get them?
- *Local schools/colleges*: relations can be developed that provide a ready supply of inexpensive and inexperienced labour. However this requires in-company training of recruits to make them effective; how do you select young people with no work experience?

- *National newspapers*: reach a large target group, but advertising is expensive and may produce a huge response.
- *Local newspapers/radio*: reaches the people in your locality but may not reach the applicants with the skills you require.
- *Specialist journals*: will guarantee you reach precisely the right group of candidates. However professional staff come at a premium. Could other experienced people (not qualified) do the job instead?
- *Recruitment consultants*: have large numbers available on their books but are rather like estate agents – if they send the details out enough times eventually someone will buy.
- *Search consultants*: anonymous, professional 'head-hunters' will handle the whole process. However they usually charge 30 per cent of the starting salary and are only used for senior positions.

Another approach to attracting candidates is to develop recruitment brochures or packs. Usually only produced by larger companies, information about the company and the job is presented in glossy folders. Brochures are normally used in markets where demand exceeds supply, such as graduate recruitment in the UK – where graduates from the 'better' universities are very much in demand.

Advertising

One of the principles of recruitment advertising is the quantity versus quality argument. Do you want an advertisement that will create a very large response that you can sort through or will you be very clear about exactly what skills and abilities are required and go for quality?

All advertisements should be accurate, informative, non-discriminatory and appealing. Essential information should be provided, such as the name of the organisation, salary, benefits, person specification and how to apply. Compare advertisement placed in your local paper with those put into specialist publications.

Handling Applications

Applications normally come in two modes:

- CVs prepared by the applicant.
- Application forms prepared by the recruiter.

CVs are usual for professional and technical positions and applications are normally favoured for more junior positions. Application forms do have an advantage in that applicants are required to provide information that is pertinent to the categories you specify and in the order you desire. This can be very useful for conducting interviews. If the original job specification has been prepared well and the advertising method is clear then handling applications should be fairly straightforward.

Selection

Selection can be broken down into three methods that can be used in isolation or to complement each other. The approach taken will depend on the culture of the organisation, and the resources available in terms of cost, time and people. The three approaches are:

- Interviews
- Tests
- Other selection methods

Interviews

Webster (1964), states that (1) decisions are made in the first three or four minutes of the interview and the rest of the time is spent supporting that decision, (2) interviewers seldom change the opinion gained from the application form, (3) interviewers place attention on the negative and (4) the behaviour of the interviewer usually betrays their decision.

Interviews are notorious for being subjective but they are the most common selection method. Often ritual behaviour is exhibited on both sides but it is important for the interviewer and the interviewee to 'like' each other. Interviewers and applicants often feel that face-to-face contact is a fitting way to be judged and it allows for an assessment of social and communication skills. In many ways interviews provide an example of ritualised behaviour. There are ritualised ways for both parties to act. Interviewees who are too pushy or assertive are automatically rejected because they are supposed to be subservient and deferential to the interviewer, who is in a position of power. Interviews often take the form of one of three stereotypes.

- *Stressful*: developed by the American Special Forces during the Second World War, such interviews try *not* to set interviewees at ease so that it can be seen how they cope in stressful situations. The technique is clearly very subjective but the basic premise is still very popular. I am not sure how useful this technique is for any job other than special forces.

- *Biographical*:   this is the normal interview where the applicants' details are discussed and explained in an orderly fashion in an attempt to be as objective as possible. A chronological sequence is usually followed.
- *Problem-solving*:   this method involves setting a task – usually related to the actions required in the job – for the interviewee to attempt.

Stressful and biographical interviews can be carried out by one or two individuals or by a panel.

Suggested approach

The best results are obtained from as objective an approach as possible. A basic approach would be:

- *Preparation*: study in advance the job description, the person specification and the Application form. Prepare a suitable venue for the interview.
- *Encounter*: recruitment is a two-way exercise. Interviewees need to understand the organisation and the position on offer. The interviewer needs to get to know the interviewees and check whether they can meet the requirements of the job.
- *Follow up*: make a decision based on the evidence, eliminating prejudice and preconception as far as possible.

Testing

Tests ensure a systematic approach but the test has to be appropriate for the job and applicant. Logically there is no job for which some test can not be devised to predict future success.

The first level of test is the *skill* test. This may involve the applicant carrying out a part of the job or conducting an appropriate simulation. In the case of secretaries it is usual to give them a spelling and typing test.

Intelligence tests tend to be used for management or graduates. Performance at verbal reasoning or mathematical tests will indicate a level of intelligence, or IQ. Particular care should be taken that these tests are not discriminatory. An English reading test may disadvantage some applicants – if the position is for, say, an unskilled worker, is it really relevant to have an intelligence type test at all?

More advanced intelligence tests may involve an 'in-tray' exercise where the recipient has to sort a selection of items in an in-tray into a logical order.

Psychological Testing is still a relatively new science. The most frequently used are psychometric assessments. These are tests that have been validated statistically, hence psychometric. They normally involve forced pair comparison, which establishes preferences and is therefore a personality indicator. One of the longer established examples is the Myers Briggs type indicator. This test places people into a system of 16 categories:

- Introvert   or extrovert
- Objective   or intuitive
- Logical   or emotional
- Decisive and purposeful or hesitant and reflective

For the best results psychometric tests should not be used in isolation but used to verify an hypothesis formulated at the interview.

An area where psychological assessments are used are assessment centres. The best example is the British Civil Service, which has been using assessment centres since the 1940s. Candidates at assessment centres are likely to receive a mixture of psychological assessments, psychometric assessments and group exercises. The benefit of the assessment centre is that multiple techniques are used.

Other selection methods

Methods that are unusual or even unorthodox are not necessarily inaccurate. The use of some methods will depend on the culture of the external environment and the culture of the organisation. A few examples are listed below:

- *Graphology*: the use of handwriting to predict personality. In continental Europe it is used very widely but it is not popular in the UK.

- *Astrology:* 'There is no known link between the position of the heavenly bodies, light years away, and the ability of someone to do the job' (Smith *et al.*, 1989).
- *Lie detectors*: polygraphs have been used, particularly in the US, to assess staff in front-line customer jobs. Applicants can be asked if they have ever stolen from an employer. Lie detectors have been shown to be manipulable, indeed in 1988 President Reagan sponsored a law banning their use in preemployment screening.

Smith, Gregg and Andrews, in *Selection and Assessment: A New Approach* (1989), have conducted some research in this area. They come up with a statistical analysis combining the results from many small studies. The authors point out that results should be 'interpreted with care' as the analysis of the result is not an exact science. However, the analysis is worth considering.

- Assessment centres and structured interviews give predictions in the 0.6s (against a perfect prediction of 1.0).
- Personality tests and unstructured interviews are in the 0.3s.
- References achieve 0.13 and Astrology and Graphology are down there with chance prediction at 0.

(A reminder of the validity of astrology as a predictive tool is the complete lack of accuracy (or severe generalisation) achieved by predictors of the National Lottery.)

Selection methods should always be validated. The most common methods are:

- Three or six month probationary period – assessment.
- An annual performance appraisal, either at a fixed time in the year or after one year of employment.
- Other more sophisticated follow-up techniques involving extensive interviews with the manager and the new recruit.

Selection Decision Making

The assessment of candidates should be completed after the interview or interviews. The employing manager, the human resource professionals (and any other managers involved in the selection) should meet to discuss the applicants. Applicants should be compared against the job description and person specification previously formulated and discussions should be objective, based on the notes taken by the interviewers during or immediately after the interview. One approach is to award points against the items covered in the job specification. That is, 1 = poorly meets the requirement, 5 = exactly meets the requirement. The candidate with the highest score will be the one to be selected when several candidates are equal or close in score or suitability. In the unlikely event that two candidates have the same score, then the candidates can be compared against each other.

Monitoring the Success of the Recruitment Process

As mentioned in the section on selection, the new employee should be assessed for suitability. It is also important for human resource professionals to analyse the methods used. Sample analysis should be made of advertising response and cost per candidate. For example, a large response to a press advertisement may seriously increase the workload in the department that has to sift the applications and respond to all the applicants. One of the benefits of using employment agencies is that there is usually a guarantee. If an employee leaves within, say, eight weeks, a full refund is available. Twelve weeks gives a 50 per cent, refund and so on. Different vacancies will require different approaches.

Induction

Having selected and recruited suitable people to join the organisation it is imperative to integrate them into the company as effectively as possible. An effective induction programme will:

- Introduce new starters to the culture of the organisation.
- Provide information on terms, benefits, evacuation points and other important information.
- Allow new starters to meet others in a similar position.
- Identify any training required to ensure that the new employees will become productive as soon as possible.

COMPETENCY BASED SELECTION

An approach to selection that has gained a lot of popularity recently is the competency approach. Until I saw it demonstrated I was quite sceptical about it. Like most people involved in recruitment I had been brought up to follow the 'biographical' and follow an interviewee's life and career in a chronological fashion. I was aware that often we would be talking about work in a very general way, then I would write my impressions down and this would form the basis of my decision making. The competency approach requires much more detailed preparation and better directed questions.

The place to start with competencies is to decide what competencies you are looking for and to what depth. This calls for a detailed job analysis and leads to a more structured approach. It is usual for tests of relevant skill and intelligence to be incorporated into the selection system. So, for example, if we take a clerical job requiring some keyboard skills to enter information onto a database and maintenance of a 'hard' filing system we can test competence at both these areas.

Having decided what the competencies are that we wish to test for, a detailed analysis of the application form will reveal areas of previous experience we can probe. Let us imagine that one of the competencies for the clerical job is getting on with people or working as part of a team. We would need to question the interviewee about experience in this area. We might want to follow up with questions about when conflict arose in the team and how the interviewee coped with that.

The difference I am trying to put across over the traditional biographical, chronological interview is that with the latter we meander through someone's career and when we get to something interesting we stop for a while. With the competency approach it is much more directed. If you are interviewing for evidence on, say, six competencies you have to manage your time to uncover information on all six. If you do not you will not acquire enough information to make an informed decision. Interviewers need to take careful notes and rate candidates against clear criteria (see later in this section).

The purpose of the interview, then, is to gain enough evidence to be able to make an informed decision. To achieve this you will need to be

precise and specific in your approach and concentrate on what the interviewee has actually done, not on the interviewee's opinions and
methods of tackling hypothetical situations. (As I write this I have a
strong recollection of being asked a leading hypothetical question at a
job interview. We were talking about a particular recruitment campaign
I had been involved in. I had obviously done a very good job of selling
it to the interviewer because she said 'and this was your idea was it'?
Well, what could I say but give the answer the interviewer wanted to
hear – yes. The truth was that I was involved in the decision but more
as a junior partner.)

The interview is for the gaining of evidence. There is no time or
necessity for follow-up questions that move on to interesting but irrelevant areas. Because there is a need to gain and record evidence it really
requires two (or three) interviewers to be present so that one can take
notes while the other asks the questions.

Another competency we might test our clerical job applicant for is
ability to cope with change. One approach would be to look for evidence to support a positive approach and evidence of a negative
approach.

Evidence for a positive approach to change:

- Openness to new ideas and approaches.
- Has responded positively in the past.
- Demonstrates an ability to improvise, where appropriate.
- Is able to 'think on feet'.
- Has a positive attitude towards learning and training.

Evidence for a negative approach to change:

- Is not receptive to new ideas and approaches.
- Has not coped well with change in the past (if leaving another job,
  why?).
- Liable to panic in changed situations.
- Has an attitude that things can not be done.

The evidence gained can be used to position the interviewee on an
assessment grid (see overleaf):

	Exceptional	Above average	Meets criterion	Does not meet criterion
Test for literacy				
Test for keyboard skills				
Adapting to change				

The interviewers complete assessments as above, tie in the results from the tests and complete the assessment individually. The next step is for the interviewers to discuss their ratings and come up with a joint recommendation. At this stage it helps to have a designated 'chair'.

Competency based selection can enhance the selection process and dramatically improve interviewing in an organisation. The down side is the overall criticism of competencies – has the organisation selected the right ones, are they being interpreted in the same way and, most worrying of all are the competencies chosen those that the decision makers would like, but do not actually reflect the reality of the job?

5 Human Resource Management Strategies

This chapter will concentrate on two human resource management practices that are of real importance to any organisation: manpower planning and communication. The approach the organisation takes to these two practices will, I think show the distinction between personnel and human resource management. That is, the latter approach is a proactive way to assist the organisation to meet its objectives.

MANPOWER PLANNING

The best known definition of manpower planning is from the old Department of Employment, which defined manpower planning as 'A strategy for the acquisition, utilisation, improvement and retention of an enterprises' human resources'.

Manpower planning is a strategy that operates at both the national and organisational levels. The demographic downturn in Europe predicted for the early 1990s has forced organisations to think about the supply of new staff. (This demographic downturn was christened the 'Mrs Robinson Syndrome' because it was all about graduates and women returners.) The UK clearing banks and the National Health Service, which traditionally employ school leavers, started to find them in short supply. They were forced to consider the ubiquitous 'woman returner'. At the national level European governments are trying to adjust the number of school and higher education places to fit demand.

For the organisation the need for long-term planning is due to:

1. Organisations becoming increasingly complex and therefore requiring more specialist skills.
2. Technology producing a need for computer-literate staff and a surplus of non-computer-literate staff.
3. National skills shortages through lack of training being available nationally, or a lack of people with certain basic required skills.

4. Employment legislation making it harder for companies to dismiss staff at whim. Instead employees are being treated more like fixed assets.
5. Changes in population trends such as people moving out of the inner cities or away from areas such as South Wales.
6. Companies (or rather the individuals in them) not enjoying making staff redundant or working understaffed while new employees are found.
7. The need to respond to change.

The aims of manpower planning are to ensure that the organisation:

● Recruits and retains staff of the right quality.
● Fully utilises the staff it has.
● Can carry out any plans it has by ensuring that staff of the right quantity and quality are available when required.

The assumptions of manpower planning are:

● Resources can be best utilised if systematic and quantitative plans are made.
● Manpower planning provides a process whereby a means of likely consequences based on different plans is achieved.
● Manpower planning assists in decisions on investment in physical resources.

So, manpower planning can help organisations to plan for, and therefore manage, human resource strategies to avoid major problems. Organisations can identify problem areas before they become problems. It provides the basis for a proactive approach to human resource management.

A typical structure for implementing manpower planning can include the following five steps:

1. The corporate plan.
2. Definition of the demand.
3. Assessment of supply.
4. Producing the manpower plan.
5. Review of the manpower plan.

The Corporate Plan

The corporate plan needs to be defined or updated to outline the corporate strategy and objectives. This will then provide the guidelines for the human resource plan. For these reasons, and others, organisations need to plan a human resource strategy in the same way that a business or corporate plan is planned. Indeed the manpower plan and the corporate plan should be interrelated.

The environment within which the manpower plan will operate is achieved by gaining the involvement and support of top management. This can be achieved by establishing manpower planning as an integral part of the organisation's strategic planning activity. That is achieved by the provision of accurate and useful information.

Definition of the Demand

The starting point of assessing demand (demand forecasting, or the estimation of the manpower resources required to meet needs or demands).will be the company corporate plan. A detailed mission statement is essential for many areas of human resource management, for manpower planning it will provide the direction. The plans need to be analysed to ascertain how they will affect the human resource.

For example, it is likely that a budget for the coming year will be negotiated by a department manager that allows for wages of, say, £100000. If the current wages bill is £95000 then the department manager needs to think where the £5000 is to go. Will the manager reward all the staff equally? Do changes in technology mean that one member of the team is now invaluable and another superfluous?

In this way managers are manpower planning. A well-managed manpower planning system will help to prevent managers making decisions that may be of benefit to their department but not to the whole organisation.

Demand forecasting will require estimates from managers on trends. That is, will technology be available that will require less staff, or will certain departments need to be increased? For example, the debt collection departments of finance houses have been forced to expand due to the recession of the early 1990s. Another approach is to carry out work study analysis. That is, breaking down the constituent parts of the job and working out the cost in time and money of completing the tasks. It is also important to include short-term and long-term skills needs in planning. Another key consideration is what the company can afford.

Many organisations do not have detailed plans of where they are going or what they want to achieve, other than short-term goals of making a profit. An interaction that can help organisations to formulate plans is to get managers to answer three questions:

1. Where are we now?
2. Where do we want to be?
3. How do we get there?

With expert facilitation managers can be led through this process to question three. This is the most important part of the process as it will require managers to negotiate a jointly agreed mission. The mission will then be jointly owned and will incorporate the vision of the key decision makers. The mission will then provide a framework around which other managers lower down the structure can formulate their mission statements.

Assessment of Supply

Assessment of supply involves analysing the existing resources and the supply of these resources in the future. Supply forecasting is concerned with forecasting the people and skills that will be available from within the organisation or externally.

Internal analysis will almost certainly require a database that holds information such as gender, marital status, age, recruitment trends, overtime, temporary staff and contractors, absenteeism and so on. External information that will need to be collected will be about the labour market, other employers in the area or same sector, transport networks and the image of the company. Some of the snapshots that will be required for a manpower stocktake are:

● Labour stability: analyses of age distribution and length of service.
● Training requirements: analyses of the stock of skills and qualifications.
● Succession planning: analyses of current performance and potential for the future.

The information developed will indicate factors such as manpower flows – which departments or jobs have a high throughput of staff.

Although this information is useful for longer-term planning it will also be essential for immediate action such as reviewing the job descriptions or reevaluating problem jobs.

Producing the Manpower Plan

This is the process of matching the demand for labour with the supply available (whether internal or external). This may lead to redeployment plans, early retirement plans or staff retraining programmes. One of the outcomes is likely to be a retention plan. The retention plan will be formulated after exit interviews have been conducted and key staff identified. It is likely to concentrate on:

- Pay: making sure the staff who are key now or will be key in the future are being suitably rewarded (and therefore retained).
- Jobs: staff with high potential can be given more interesting and demanding assignments, such as project work.
- Training: training requirements may be identified to prepare key staff for future jobs.
- Commitment: showing, and telling, the ones you want to retain that they are important and have a future with the organisation.

With the use of computers it is possible to project trends from the past into the future. That is, to try to simulate what will happen in one or two years hence. The outcome could be strategies to move people between departments or cross-training them so that they can be moved into the areas of greatest need. Another approach might be to hire temporary staff as the project/work that needs to be completed will take, say, only 12 months. In that way costs can be minimised and there will not be a surplus of staff at the end of the project. Alternatively the plan may indicate that there is no need to hire staff on short-term contracts. For example in retail extra staff are required for Christmas. These staff will need to be trained. The plan could be to employ students who have worked in the organisation before. In that way you can ensure you have trained staff but there is also an incentive for the students to perform well, that is they could be offered a job the following Christmas and in their other holidays.

Another example of a company changing its traditional plans is that of Sainsbury's, the supermarket chain. When they discovered that young people were becoming unavailable they targeted the over 50s. The new staff became known as 'pensioner packers' and proved to be more reliable, trustworthy and flexible than younger staff.

Review of the Manpower Plan

The plan needs to be carefully updated and the forecasts compared with reality. For example the manpower plan analysis may produce results that indicate the corporate plan needs to be modified. Therefore feedback is an essential part of the system. The results of the plan lead to human resource management plans in other areas such as recruitment and selection and training and development.

For example, in 1989 a building society in the UK, the Alliance & Leicester, identified that the supply of young people would be reduced due to the demographic downturn. The manpower plan of the organisation still required the company to recruit 16- and 17-year-olds, but other organisations were also targeting this group. The Alliance and Leicester decided to establish high-profile links with schools and colleges and offered a business studies prize scheme. This offered prizes of money, textbooks and advice on writing CVs as well as careers and work experience opportunities.

The company also identified some staff retention measures. It found a strong link between the payment of London and South East weighting and length of service. Analysis of the external market indicated a supply of potential workers for the weekends and evenings – so working practices were changed and work identified that could be undertaken at these unconventional times.

For women who had left the workforce to have families the company provided refresher training on their return and kept in touch with them while on maternity or career-break schemes. In addition, to meet demand needs the company agreed to let older employees work past retirement age if their ability and performance were not impaired.

There is evidence that some employment practices are changing. Some flexible work patterns identified by Cooper (1990) include:

● V-Time: an option for staff to reduce their hours so that they can spend time on voluntary work (for a temporary period).

- Career-break scheme: many organisations have finally twigged to the idea that if you re-employ women who have had time off to have children they (1) will not need retraining, (2) are likely to be quite committed and (3) will be prepared to work part-time.
- Sabbaticals: employees aged over 50 and with long service are starting to be offered the chance to take six month or twelve month sabbaticals. This can give employees a chance to recharge their batteries and redefine their vision, while the organisation is afforded an opportunity to try people out in future jobs and encourage the idea that no one is indispensable.

COMMUNICATION

In a recession, we must communicate because we are working with frightened people who always fear the worst. You may only need to lose 30% of jobs, but if you do not communicate you will frighten 100% of your people as they thrive on rumours. (John Harvey-Jones, 1984)

Trainers often refer to there being three levels of communication:

- Hand to hand: the passing on of written information.
- Head to head: information passed verbally.
- Heart to heart: information passed and received at the level that it is taken on board, understood and acted upon.

Effective communication should be a goal of all organisations. Unfortunately the culture of some companies (secrecy, fear of being found out) is such that communication as a process will not function easily. Internal communication can be used, and is used, by many organisations as a method of introducing organisation change.

To help a better understanding of what is going on during communication it is useful to digress slightly to look at the formal and informal organisation.

The Formal and Informal Organisation

The formal organisation is the planned activity to meet organisation objectives and the informal organisation is the result of the interaction of the people working in the organisation.

The *formal organisation* is a combination of the culture and structure of the organisation. Individuals' roles have been set, objectives are in place, activities have been coordinated. The best representation of the formal organisation is the organisation chart showing hierarchy, spans of control and authority.

The *informal organisation* will always be present and it arises from the interactions of the organisation's members. This organisation is flexible and loosely structured. The values and norms can work against the formal organisation but the informal can be used to work for the same common goals as the formal.

Gray and Starke (1988) have developed a model that provides a comparison between the formal and informal, the key points of which are as follows:

Characteristic	Formal organisation	Informal organisation
Structure		
Origin	Planned	Spontaneous
Rationale	Rational	Emotional
Characteristics	Stable	Dynamic
Goals	Profitability (or service to Society)	Member Satisfaction
Influence		
Base	Position	Personality
Type	Authority	Power
Flow	Top down	Bottom up
Communication		
Channels	Formal	Grapevine
Networks	Follow formal lines	Cuts across regular channels
Speed	Slow	Fast
Accuracy	High	Low
Individuals included	All	Only those acceptable
Interpersonal relations	As defined by the job	Spontaneous
Basis for Interaction	Functional	Personal characteristics

Source: Gray and Starke (1988)

Formal organisations use informal organisation for two reasons: (1) to foster a sense of identity, belonging and motivation, and (2) the grapevine will always exist and it is very effective at transferring important information around the organisation.

Communication is vital in the organisation climate of the 1990s because employees need to understand:

- The mission, goals and objectives of the organisation so that they can see how they fit in.
- The standards expected of them.
- How they are performing against those standards.
- How policy decisions will affect them and how those decisions were arrived at.
- Employees also need to be given the opportunity to provide feedback and to demonstrate innovation.

Failure to communicate is costly. The costs are in time, cooperation, morale and effectiveness. The outcome is the ubiquitous 'grapevine'. Grapevines rarely operate on all the facts and in the minds of the recipients are proof that the company does not tell anyone what is going on.

The barriers to effective communication are not insurmountable. People, perhaps due to higher educational and social standards, are expecting more from their employers. Time, as a resource, is becoming more scarce – managers and supervisors are being pressed for short-term results and longer-term development is suffering. People seem to have a fear of speaking in front of their peers or staff. In the UK public speaking is not something that is practised often. Perhaps the greatest barrier to communication is organisational structure – organisations with many layers will inevitably have to pass a message a long way. The apocryphal story from the trenches of the First World War began as 'We're going to advance, send for reinforcements' and ended back at headquarters as 'we're going to a dance, send for three and fourpence'.

The value of internal communication can be expressed by two models, In Model 1, which is a picture of poor formal communication, there is a downwards spiral (Figure 5.1). A positive formal communication system can be used as an intervention in to the existing system to change it.

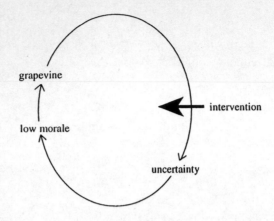

Figure 5.1   The downward spiral of poor communication

For organisations that are communicating well, an effective formal communication system can act as a barrier, as protection from extreme movements both inside and outside the organisation (Figure 5.2).

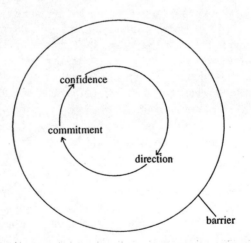

Figure 5.2   The self-fulfilling cycle of good communication practice

Internal Communication Methods

Some of the most frequently used formal, internal communication methods are:

- Noticeboards
- Magazines and newsletters
- Consultative committees
- Presentations (including video presentations)
- Staff briefing structures
- Other methods

Noticeboards

The theory is that most people look at and read noticeboards. They are often put close to coffee points or in rest rooms. The problem with them is that they tend to get filled up with witty newspaper headlines or personal items for sale. People also stop looking at them when it is usual for all the items to be out of date. The information can also be deliberately or accidentally censored. It is not uncommon for managers in remote offices to fail to put all the notified internal vacancies on the boards as they do not want to lose experienced or difficult to replace staff to head office or other local offices.

Magazines and newsletters

Many large companies run in-house magazines or newsletters. The UK clearing banks have established departments purely for the purpose of managing the in-house journal. To be successful there needs to be a balance between human interest stories and articles from management about 'real' issues or decisions. There is normally provision for staff to to publish letters expressing their views. Usually representatives are appointed from different areas of the company to collect local information that can be included.

Magazines are usually produced by management and the content is therefore controlled. Newsletters tend to be more employee generated and are not necessarily subject to management editing. Some daring companies allow all letters to be published without editing.

Consultative committees

These approaches to communication are more evident in traditionally structured organisations with a history of industrial relations. The consultative committees are constituted of management and staff to discuss matters affecting the organisation. Consultative committees are normally created around an agreed procedure and often have a formal constitution. Information is circulated onwards via formalised minutes, probably pinned on to noticeboards. These committees allow a degree of two-way communication, but not in the same way as German companies where employee representatives are required by law to be on the board.

Presentations

A popular method of communication, particularly favoured by erudite, charismatic leaders, is to hold presentations for all staff, either on a regular basis or as needs be. These can be conducted by the leader in person or on videotape. Anita Roddick of the Body Shop regularly prepares video briefings that are distributed to her stores for all staff to see. Leaders often enjoy the challenge of meeting subordinate managers and being challenged about their policy and decisions.

Unfortunately briefing large groups usually leads to no questions at all. Junior or less confident staff feel inhibited about speaking in front of their peers and managers and junior managers do not like to question decisions in case they are seen to be disloyal.

In the right context presentations can be very useful. For example, Colin Marshall, the chief executive officer of British Airways, visited 95 per cent of the management training courses run by BA under their Managing People First initiative. At each one he gave a presentation and encouraged feedback.

Staff briefing structures

One of the most commonly used staff briefing structures is that of team briefing, as developed by the Industrial Society. The concept is that information cascades down the organisation, with all staff at a particular level receiving the message at the same time. The concept is best visualised by thinking of circles of champagne glasses stacked upon each other as at a wedding. The champagne will flow evenly, filling up each level as it cascades down.

The key features, then, are:

1. As the term implies, team briefings are for work teams. The team leader conducts the briefing and teams should not be larger than 15 or smaller than four.
2. Team briefing needs to be regular – Monthly or bimonthly – and conducted systematically.
3. The information being communicated is mostly one-way – downwards. The briefing should last about 20 to 30 minutes and should not deviate into open discussion or debate.
4. The briefing should be structured such that at each level 70 per cent of the information is 'local' or directly relevant to that level. The other 30 per cent is information or messages from the higher levels of the cascade.
5. The structure, once established, can be used for exceptional items. So, for example, if an organisation takes over another or forms a joint venture then a special briefing can be called by senior management to ensure that all staff get the same message at the same time.

The Industrial Society propose that suitable subjects will fall under the four Ps:

- Progress
- Policy
- People
- Points for Action

Some samples of items typically included are listed below (these are taken from a series of workshops with managers in a financial services company in the UK, who presented lists of suitable items).

Progress	*Policy*
Business results	Company mission statement
New business	Redundancy policy
IT developments	Personnel policies generally, for
Business plans	example pay, holidays, and
	so on

Advertising campaigns
Acquisitions/
   joint ventures
Performance of market/
   competitors

Health and safety
Marketing policy
Training and development policy
Employee suggestion scheme

People

Staff changes – starters/
   leavers/transfers
Job vacancies
External achievements by
   individuals
First aiders and fire
   wardens
Weddings, babies, and so on
Résumés of key people

Points for Action

Visitors to the building
Health and safety
Sports and social club events
Holiday cover
Use of temporary staff
System changes
Housekeeping

Team briefing does have some disadvantages. If news is light the temptation is to cancel a briefing at short notice or fill it with trivial items. The messages from the top can be misinterpreted. One London organisation announced that the staff restaurant, which was opened for breakfast, would close at 8.45 am so that all staff could be at work at 9 am. The message may have been very well intentioned but it came over as being very condescending and in an environment of looser management control and more freedom for individuals to act could have been seen as reminiscent of 'Big Brother'.

Another problem is that if some areas do not take it seriously then the whole edifice can start to crumble. The very structured nature of team briefing also supports the hierarchy. Managers with only one or two staff end up being briefed and then briefing onwards themselves, simply because they are managers at a certain level, when they could be briefed more efficiently all together.

The obverse of that situation is managers who call large departments or divisions together. The group becomes one of very mixed ability. Managers may be reluctant to ask searching questions in front of junior staff and staff may not want to look stupid in front of management.

Other communication methods

Other methods exist that are more ephemeral or are not communication strategies but have an impact on communication.

Attitude surveys. Attitude surveys can have a dramatic short-term effect on staff morale and communication. They test the opinion and attitudes of all staff on a variety of issues. They are particularly used to highlight areas of concern to staff that management can act upon. So, communication may be an issue, or the benefits package and so on. The very act of conducting an attitude survey makes people communicate. The downside is that if nothing happens after the survey, staff can become disillusioned and see the whole exercise as a waste of time.

Suggestion schemes. Although these schemes produce ideas to make the company more effective, managers are fond of using them as a means of opening up communication, of encouraging staff to talk about ideas.

For a practical example of communication training see Chapter 11 on empowerment, where I describe a communication and influencing skills workshop that I have been running for organisations as part of empowerment programmes.

6 Training and Development

Training and development are key activities for all organisations. The organisation may decide to use its own trainers or buy in specialist skills. Either way training serves a variety of purposes. For example, it can be used to motivate people: send them on a course to show them how much the organisation loves them. It can also be used as a form of punishment: some people are not sent on the training courses they need or qualify for, or they are sent on courses in areas where they are competent but perhaps made a small mistake. The organisation, in the form of a particular boss, is trying to tell them something.

Training can serve as a reward. In some companies you qualify for a week-long management skills training at places such as Ashridge when you reach a certain grade. You might not have any staff to manage but it is one of the perceived rewards of the grade (along with the company car).

Some of the more positive reasons for training are:

- To add value to the existing 'stock' of employees by developing them.
- Rapid changes in systems due to technology may mean that staff need to be kept up to date.
- A need for greater customer responsiveness and speed of action.
- To increase the motivation and commitment of staff.
- To ensure that staff in new jobs become fully competent as soon as possible.
- Responding to rapid change in the world-wide business environment.
- To improve individual, team and corporate performance.

In a recent speech Lee McKee, the personnel director of Woolworths, quoted a PE international survey suggesting that against key performance indicators the largest UK companies outperform their European counterparts. He reported a positive correlation between increased training expenditure and enhanced productivity and profitability.

THE TRAINING CYCLE

For training to be effective it is important that a systematic process is followed. This is usually called the training cycle. The four steps of the cycle are:

1. Identifying training needs.
2. Formulating how the need will be satisfied.
3. Implementing the training.
4. Evaluating training effectiveness.

The process is necessarily a system as each step leads into the other, including going back to step 1 from step 4:

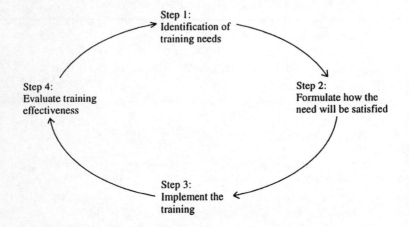

Step 1:
Identification of
training needs

Step 2:
Formulate how the
need will be satisfied

Step 3:
Implement the
training

Step 4:
Evaluate training
effectiveness

This cycle is influenced by the *external environment*. The external environment could be the culture of the organisation, the educational system in operation in the country, or national considerations such as legislation and factors such as a social charter.

In some countries, for example, France, Singapore and Australia, employers have to spend a percentage of payroll costs on training (3 per cent, 2 per cent, and 1.5 per cent respectively). This is one explanation of why so many Europeans speak English – their employers send them on language training courses for two reasons: to improve their English, and because it is an easy way to comply with the training requirements.

The Ford Motor company has long had a culture of promoting training and runs a scheme called the Employee Development and Assistance Programme (EDAP). This scheme is not job-related, what it is about is empowerment – the empowerment of individuals who wish to develop themselves. The EDAP scheme gives grants to individuals to attend courses on subjects such as foreign languages, stopping smoking, learning to drive or underwater photography. The EDAP grant from the company to the employee can be up to £200. Figures show that over half of Ford's UK workforce of 30 000 have taken part. Ford has created a culture where learning and training have a high priority. The pay-off for Ford must be that staff who are interested in self-development will be more motivated and committed to the organisation.

Another UK company with a positive learning culture is Unipart. The Unipart approach is more directly related to business issues: 'this morning's training should be applicable to this afternoon's job'. The company has renamed its training centre 'the University' and the library 'the Learning Curve'. A third of the staff have attended compulsory courses. The MD's commitment is that he speaks regularly on courses being run.

Step 1: Identification of Training Needs

A training need is an existing or anticipated shortfall or problem in performance where training is considered the most appropriate and effective solution. It can also be thought of as the 'gap' between what is happening and what should be happening.

Identifying needs properly is obviously a very important part of the training cycle. If your analysis is wrong at this stage then the later training activity will also be inappropriate. This may result in wasting money and demotivating staff. It can also set up negative attitudes towards future training. It is important that the training objectives are clearly stated so that the results of the training can be clearly evaluated

Training needs can be identified at the individual and the organisation level. At the *individual level*:

1. Identification will need to begin with the job description. This will provide a list of the skills and knowledge required. It can be compared with the actual skills and knowledge that the job holder possesses.

2. Another approach could be to look at critical incidents over, say, the past three months that were particularly challenging or stressful. The training can then be directed at the areas that are most relevant.
3. Managers will also be able to identify training for their subordinates. One of the best ways of achieving this is through the appraisal interview, where agreed training needs can be identified.
4. Individuals may request training that they perceive will equip them for a change of job, either laterally or through promotion.

At the organisation level:

1. Training needs may be identified through the performance appraisal system. This may provide the key channel for feeding back individual needs. The information should be processed by a human resource professional in order to plan the overall needs of the organisation.
2. The management team or a training committee (if one is established) may identify areas from the corporate plan that they want included in the training plans. So, for example, an organisation that is planning to expand may want all supervisors to be properly trained in supervisory techniques, including recruitment and selection. Alternatively management may identify a short-term problem in one area and dictate that extra training be provided. An example may be of a department that is constantly not completing tasks due to overrunning. A short-term response could be to provide time management training. This may not be the complete solution as poor time management may be a symptom of an underlying problem, but it will help to make the department more efficient.

Training needs analysis – the practice

Training needs analysis can be examined with respect to two groups – jobs and people.

Jobs.   The first question to ask is: what are the training priorities? The answers may lie in the manpower plan or in the importance of the problem to the organisation. The next stage is to consider how the job can best be analysed. This could involve observation, questioning or job analysis.

People. Analysis will reveal the kind of person required. Information can be used from the person specification. (For more information on job descriptions see Chapter 4 on recruitment and selection.)

How to identify training needs

In this section we will look at three different methods of how you might go about the actual process of identifying training needs. The three methods are:

- The fully comprehensive review.
- The priority problem approach.
- The performance management approach.

The fully comprehensive review. A comprehensive organisation-wide review might follow the following four steps:

- Step 1: preparing for the review. Obtain a clear brief and support from the top management. Explain the purpose of the review to all those involved in order to enlist their support and, hopefully, avoid any 'uncooperative' attitudes.
- Step 2: collection of data and initial interpretation; identification of problems with non-training solutions. Collect information on the following:
  - External influences such as changes in demand or technological innovations.
  - Top management objectives. This might be information from the corporate plan and information from the top management on changes they see coming.
  - The human resource. Such information might be available in the manpower plan. Other information that will be useful will be information on recruitment plans, selection policy, assessment systems and promotion policy.
  - The views of line management. Line managers will know about the existing practices and their adequacy. Information may be available on specific jobs where gaps in knowledge or skill are producing poor performance. Line managers should also have ideas on future training needs and the priorities of their departments.

- Step 3: detailed Interpretation of data; Identification of key areas; development of recommendations. At this stage it should be possible to rank training priorities. This can be accomplished at department level and then organisation level. Linking back to step 2 the training plan should support the corporate plan and objectives. It should be acceptable to all levels of management and to those receiving the training. The plan will be practical and costed.
- Step 4: implement the recommendations. Acceptance by top management of all or part of the recommendations will lead to the formulation of detailed training programmes and plans.

The priority problem approach.   This approach, as the name implies, involves concentrating on the organisation's urgent problems. This approach is ad hoc but still systematic. Concentration is on areas that are critical to the organisation's objectives. The emphasis is definitely short-term.

The performance management approach.   This approach looks at appraisal and performance management from the training perspective. (See Chapter 8 on performance management.)

As an approach this is the one that will lead easiest into a 'learning organisation' – one where it is accepted that everyone is still learning. Because of environmental change the organisation is constantly changing, therefore the jobs in the organisation are constantly changing and individuals need to be constantly learning new skills in order to keep up.

In this approach managers and staff jointly set and review performance objectives, and therefore identify training and development needs on a continuous basis. The responsibility for identifying training needs is very clearly with line management. Indeed, training will become an integral part of management's responsibility. The role of the training consultant can become that of an internal consultant. This approach requires as its bedrock line managers having detailed and relevant job descriptions for their staff so that they can see the training gaps.

Step 2: Meeting Training Needs

Formulating how the needs can be met can be carried out in different ways.

Training policies

A proactive way of writing training into the practices of an organisation is to develop and communicate a training policy. The policy will reinforce the culture of the organisation – or the new culture if planned organisation change is being implemented. The training policy will also provide a framework within which training can operate. For example, the following lays down the philosophy and aims of a training and development policy for a financial services company in the city:

Philosophy

The .... Training and Development policy is based on the belief that people enjoy learning. It assumes that people do not need to be cajoled or coaxed into undertaking training or development activities – that they naturally seek to increase their work based knowledge and to enhance their technical skills, in order to develop themselves and to maximise job satisfaction.

As an employer, we believe that investment in an individual's training and development should be in the interests of both the individual and the company.

We also believe that we need to learn as a company. X ... must learn to continually adapt itself in order to meet the new challenges it faces in the market place. A company can only learn if its people learn and pass on their wisdom. We believe that our Training and Development strategies will help to provide us with the necessary feedback from staff, to ensure that we stay ahead of our competitors in terms of the speed and quality of our response to new opportunities.

Aims

1   To train all staff to carry out their present job effectively and efficiently.
2   To develop those staff who have the potential to move across jobs or to take on increased responsibility as and when required by the Company.
3   To offer all staff the opportunity to keep up-to-date on matters which affect them, that is, changes and developments within the Company and the marketplace.
4   To spend the training budget prudently to ensure maximum return in terms of Company performance.

Planned training interventions

Training interventions need to be designed carefully to ensure that they meet the identified needs. The following are a guide to some of the issues that need to be considered in designing training.

Objectives. The objectives need to be considered against the desired end results. The end result will be the acquisition of a new skill or changed behaviour. Skills and behaviours can be learned. A skill can be learnt in isolation whereas a behavioural change will lead to permanent change in the values and behaviours held. That means, teaching the skill of juggling to people who can not juggle is achievable.

Location. Is the training to be on-site? Is the training to be run by an external source?

Timing. Is there an optimum time for the training to take place? What is the duration of the training, and if it is to be a series of courses does a pilot course need to be planned?

Level. If the training is to be conceptual only are the trainees experienced enough to be able to relate it to the work situation?

Techniques. Consideration should be given to elements of technique. Is it appropriate to use case studies or role plays? What is the objectivity level of the trainer and the expectation of the trainee?

Learning theory

It is useful here to digress slightly and spend some time on learning theory. Fitts (1965) suggests three different stages of *skill acquisition*:

● *Cognitive assimilation of information:* this is the concept that trainees can learn as much by actually doing or practising a task as they can by being shown how to do it or given theoretical instruction. An example might be making/baking a cake.
● *Associative:* the idea that frequent repetition of a task results in progressively better performance. This increase in performance can be slow and progressive. An example might be playing golf (although

my father tells me that his slow progress is so slow it is almost non-existent).

- *Automatisation of responses:* driving is a good example of this process. For learners there is a great deal of new information to be taken in and new skills to be learnt. When learners have become experienced they are able to concentrate more on monitoring overall performance, picking up potential future hazards or even admiring the scenery!

Another way of approaching learning is to think of it as a process that starts with being unaware that training is needed and ends with full competence:

- Unconscious incompetence: I don't know what I don't know.

A certain 16-year-old can not drive and is used to getting lifts and buses. None of the young person's peers drive, it is not part of their mind-set. It is just not an issue.

- Conscious incompetence: I am aware that I don't know how to do something. Possibly, an individual will want to do something about this incompetence.

Our young person is now a year older and some friends have learnt to drive. The perception is that those friends who can drive and can borrow their parents' cars are able to attract boyfriends/girlfriends more easily. There is a strong desire to change the non-driving situation.

- Conscious competence: I have learnt how to do certain skills but while they are new I have to concentrate quite hard.

Learning to drive is a painful process. For the first few months (and a lot longer for some people) it is quite a task to remember everything and drive. Finding the right gear, remembering to look at the mirrors, following a route – all complex tasks.

- Unconscious competence: I can ride my bicycle without falling off and am able to observe the countryside and watch out for motorists, who are very inconsiderate to cyclists.

Our driver is now 18 years old and drives every day. The young adult is able to drive without really having to think about the procedures required. Fiddling with the radio or letting the mind wander on motorway journeys detracts little from performance.

Learning styles

David Kolb (1984) has developed a very important theory of learning called 'experiential learning'. Experiences are what we go through in order to learn. As individuals we learn more from some experiences than others. The learning process is as follows:

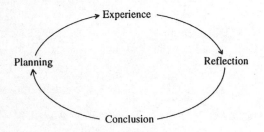

- *Experience*: we have an experience.
- *Reflection*: if we analyse this experience we can learn from our successes and failures.
- *Conclusion*: at this stage we begin to make sense of the learning by relating it to other ideas or experiences we have had.
- *Planning*: we start to do things differently as a result of having gone through this process.

Honey and Mumford (1986) have developed a similar classification (and a very good questionnaire to help you to place yourself). The following descriptions of the learning styles may give you some idea of what your preferred learning style is. It will also give you an idea of what parts of the learning process you are weaker at.

- *Activist*: activists absorb themselves fully in new experiences and tend to jump in at the deep end. They are open minded, enthusiastic, gregarious, flexible and thrive on challenge. The downside to this approach is that they act first and consider the consequences afterwards. They have 'butterfly' attention spans – they get bored quickly and want to move on to the next activity.
- *Reflector*: these people like to stand back and take it all in. They may take a minor role in discussions but will assimilate other people's ideas readily. They are likely to be thoughtful and methodical and will demonstrate good listening skills. The weaknesses of

this approach are that they are reluctant to participate, may be cautious and are endlessly revisiting the past.

- *Theorist*: these people are able to integrate their observations into theories or patterns. They will be logical, rational, objective and disciplined. The disadvantages of this style are that theorists have a low tolerance of chaos, they will probably have a tendency towards perfectionism and an intolerance of intuition and subjectivity.
- *Pragmatist*: pragmatists like to put theories and concepts in to practice. They like new ideas and will seek them out and test them. These people are likely to be practical and realistic. The weaknesses could be that these types are task-oriented and they like to get on with things without always testing the options.

Being aware of our dominant style or styles may help us to select the most appropriate training activities.

Individual learning

Individual learning can take place in one of three broad categories. The method used will depend on the culture of the organisation. The three categories are:

- Formal education and training.
- Group learning.
- Assignment or planned experience.

Formal education and training. Learning will only take place if the recipient wants to learn. There can be several reasons for the block (that is, not wanting to learn): employees may be sent on courses that are not directly relevant to them; they may be put on courses that they would not have chosen for themselves; they may have legitimate reasons for not wishing to spare the time or the expense; and possibly the objectives of the course have not been explained very well. On the other hand there are courses that staff are put on when they reach a certain level in the hierarchy – the course becomes a means of heightening self-esteem and prestige.

Learning also takes place within a context. For example, when seen out of context friends or acquaintances are often difficult to place. In the same way formal learning that takes place in a 'cultural island' may not be readily used by the individual.

Effective learning is also learning that is 'owned'. Learning by rote or memorising facts needs to be continually practised or it is learning that is not easily transferable. Discovery learning lasts longer. This is learning where individuals discover knowledge for themselves.

Group learning.   The quality of the learning will depend on the group. A group that is fully formed and has a high appreciation of training will learn more than a group that does not. The most effective group within which to learn will be the work group. Not all work groups, though, will have a positive training culture.

Assignment or planned experience.   Learning needs to be put into practice. Experiences on their own will not lead to changed behaviour. A current theory, borrowed from the Ancient Greeks, is that the starting point for understanding others and changing our own behaviour is to understand ourselves. That is, why we do things, why we believe what we believe. Armed with this understanding it is possible for individuals to plan the training they require, and be able to help other people solve their problems without their own problems getting in the way. In the Greek city of Athens, which was renowned for its civilisation, education was of paramount importance. Above the entrance to the University of Athens were inscribed the words 'Know Thyself.' Plato, in *The Republic*, described education as turning 'the mind's eye to the light, so that it can see for itself'.

Organisations with a positive training culture appreciate that individuals make mistakes and that these are learning opportunities. A learning organisation is one that encourages risk taking. Allied to this the organisation has to make clear the objectives or expectations it has. Handy (1987) suggests that if an organisation believes that its managers can perform effectively, they will perform effectively if allowed to do so. This high expectation creates a self-fulfilling prophecy. That is, if we believe that we are effective we will behave in a way that reinforces that belief. Other people will see our behaviour and consider that because we act so confidently then perhaps we are effective. The other person will therefore treat us in such a way, recognising our competence, that we assume we are right to behave the way we do. We have then had our approach verified as one that deserves respect, so we continue. Unfortunately under self-fulfilling prophecy it is also possible to act in a way that could be considered negative.

The concept of the self-fulfilling prophecy is one that is used to underpin assertiveness training. Assertiveness skills help us to break the existing self-fulfilling prophecies that reinforce our position as passive or aggressive. When we put into place assertive behaviour, this, by virtue of the self-fulfilling prophecy, is reinforced.

Modelling is another effective learning method. We can learn by modelling ourselves on others who exhibit the right behaviour and practices.

Adult learners

Training within organisations is almost exclusively aimed at adult learners. So it would seem useful at this point to think a bit about what that means, and how we can design and conduct training in ways that will make it acceptable and beneficial to adult learners.

The starting point is to think a little about what their previous experiences of training have been like. The place to start is their schooling. I find, from the various seminars and workshops that I run, that many people have had bad experiences in the education system. Learning was not fun, it was all too often associated with punishment, being pilloried for getting things wrong. Many adults can recall one particular teacher in one subject who made that subject come alive, and their lessons interesting. School experiences are often of very large groups where individuals were reluctant to speak up and could be left unattended. With all this 'baggage' of bad experiences it is not surprising that people come to training as adults with low self-confidence and low self-image.

All these prior events come together in the form of fear. Longman (1991), in their developing training skills programme, have drawn together some truths about fear.

- The only way to get rid of the fear of doing something is to go out and do it.
- Not only am I going to experience fear whenever I'm on unfamiliar territory, but so is everyone else.
- Pushing through fear is less frightening than living with the underlying fear that comes from a feeling of helplessness.

Some of the techniques that can help adults to learn are:

- Relating the learning to actual problems they are experiencing.
- Linking the learning to their own goals or visions.
- Giving the adults some control over decisions that have to be made. For example some trainers that I have worked with find it very difficult to let delegates work in small groups of the delegates' choosing. The trainers see their position as one of power and they want to control everything that happens. Setting ground rules at the beginning of training courses is also a good opportunity to allow delegates some control.
- Encouraging participation, that is, encouraging all delegates to participate without judging their contribution. This basically means the facilitator needs to listen with interest and empathy.
- Fun: learning can be fun. I strongly believe that if trainers are not enjoying their work or do not believe in what they are teaching then the delegates will find it hard to take in as well. Examples of fun could be activities such as 'ice-breakers' or other exercises. Ice-breakers are small group exercises that are used as a bit of fun at the start of the course, or when delegates appear to be wilting. A good example is getting the group members to arrange themselves in order of height or age. Other exercises are activities such as Lego building, which encourages team building or leadership skills (see later in this chapter).
- Using the experience of adults to highlight points. In school, schoolchildren do not always have experiences that they can draw on. Therefore the teacher is seen as the expert who can transfer knowledge to the students. Often the challenge for trainers with adult learners is to get the learners to understand that the trainer does not have all the answers. The trainer can help the learners to tap into the reservoir of their own experiences.

Step 3: Implementing Training

The approaches that can be used fall broadly into 'on the job' and 'off the job' techniques. Some training techniques cross the barriers. Some 'on the job' techniques are as follows.

Job rotation. This technique is moving staff to a job in a different function, product or activity.

Job enrichment. Stretching the boundaries or requirements of the existing job by allocating additional responsibilities or tasks.

Secondment. Transferring the individual to another job for a fixed period. A good example of a secondment is the practice of taking managers out of the 'line' and making them training officers. Clearly individuals have to be chosen carefully and it has to be something they want to do.

Special projects. Giving individuals responsibility for a special project outside the normal routines of their current jobs. An example might be charging someone, or a group of people, with organising the Christmas party.

Working parties or special subcommittees. Staff can be put in special groups to tackle a problem or come up with suggestions on a subject they may know something about but is not part of their job. Examples could be reviewing the company appraisal scheme or participating in a training subcommittee.

Coaching. Deliberately working individuals through problems or new areas of expertise.

Mentoring. Establishing a relationship with a more senior manager (this is also called 'grandparenting') who can provide guidance, advice and feedback. The mentor might let the subject sit in on senior policy-making committees or involve them in the process of making organisation-wide decisions.

Planned experience. Establishing certain new skills the individual will learn over the next six months; ensuring that the training takes place, and that the skills are learned.

'Off the job' techniques include the following.

Lectures.   Attending lectures to keep up to date, either open lectures or professional institute ones. In the UK the Law Society require solicitors to keep their knowledge up to date (professional development). One way of doing this is to attend external lectures or courses approved by the Law Society. The Society awards points for each seminar/lecture attended. A practising lawyer or solicitor must 'clock up' so many points per year. Many professional institutions, such as the Institute of Personnel and Development, offer programmes of lectures.

Group discussions.   These can be run in isolation or as part of other training initiatives such as lectures.

Clinics.   Specialists in certain topics might offer individuals the opportunity to work on a specific area.

Individual tutorials.   A specialist may be required to work with an individual on a one-off basis. Examples, might be preparation for an important presentation or individual tutoring in a foreign language.

Films.   Films can provide a very good learning medium. They are perhaps more useful as part of a training initiative. John Cleese, the comedian, and Video Arts, a UK company, produce a whole series of training films that are comical in approach. They take, for example, a subject such as appraisal interviewing and show several versions of how it should not be conducted. This approach has been criticised as it does not always show trainees an example of how the interview should be conducted properly. Funny films can be effective though, as the trainees tend to find them amusing and to remember the stereotypes.

Simulations.   In some occupations simulations are a very effective training method. Flight simulators, for example, allow pilots to practice without endangering themselves or expensive equipment. Other forms of simulation include case studies, such as the in-tray exercises used in selection for recruitment or promotion, and business games. Perhaps the best known UK business game is the ICL-Cranfield management game. Teams of four or five are given information about a company and have to make decisions about how the company should progress, that is, mass produce widgets and sell them at a low price or hand-make them and sell them at a high price. Often the trainees will learn as much from the experience of working with other staff from the same company as they will from the game.

Role plays.   These offer an opportunity to practice skills in a safe environment in as near to real situations as possible. It is possible to video-record episodes and play them back to delegates so that they can evaluate their performance. Individuals can play either themselves or the other party in the incident. For example, by playing the part of the person they need to discipline, appraise or whatever, they can learn a lot about the feelings involved and see it from the other's point of view.

An example of the use of role playing is one from a company in London. A manager wanted to discipline a member of his team who had a poor attendance record and whose standard of work had been deteriorating. The member of staff actually had a debilitating illness called ME, which leaves sufferers tired, lethargic and feeling generally unwell. The manager concerned found it very instructive to role play the person and to experience the feelings associated with having a disease that was not taken seriously. The manager experienced the feeling of being accused of not caring or showing enough enthusiasm when actually it was the illness that had stopped the employee from staying late at work and looking enthusiastic.

Reading.   All people have the opportunity to read books and articles about their area of work or the skills involved. Many people who use public transport take the opportunity to read while commuting into work.

Distance learning.   Some disciplines are learnt easily by distance learning or correspondence courses. The disadvantage is that trainees do not get the opportunity to discuss the work with their peers and some subjects are easier than others to learn in isolation.

Computer based training/interactive video.   CBT is fast becoming a popular means of studying. Usually a trainee is given a choice of questions and progresses through the programme by answering the right ones. The Stock Exchange in London runs a series of administrative examinations. The course work is carried out in a course book and the one-hour examination is taken at a computer terminal and consists of multiple choice questions.

Training courses and workshops

Training courses and workshops are an off-the-job technique that require special consideration. They offer an opportunity to impart concentrated knowledge, and skills can be learnt or practised in a safe environment. Courses permit individuals to leave the day-to-day demands of their jobs behind so that they can concentrate on analysing past behaviours and reflecting on what has been successful and what has not. Training courses also provide an opportunity to introduce change, either through the introduction of new ideas or through peer group pressure whereby the 'odd ones out' can see the behaviours adopted by their peers.

Internal training courses.   An important part of any internal training course is that it allows staff to meet for the first time people working in other parts of the same organisation. Knowledge of the organisation is therefore increased, barriers are broken down and a sense of identification or belonging is increased. Effective internal courses should be highly participative and action based. Delegates should go away with action points to put into practice. Armstrong (1991), lists three essential characteristics for effective internal courses:

1. They should be problem-based: the course should help delegates to overcome actual problems that are a barrier to better performance.
2. Action orientated: the course should result in specific action that produces improvements in actual performance and the improvements should be easily monitored.
3. Senior management: the involvement and support of senior managers is essential. By demonstrating recognition of the course, senior management is making a statement about the importance of training, the need constantly to improve performance and the interrelationship of the two. Culture is clearly an important factor here. Some organisations have a culture that all training should be provided externally or by external consultants. Other organisations have a very xenophobic approach to training and only use internal trainers.

External training courses. External courses often have an unsettling effect; people go away and learn new skills and approaches and when they return they have no opportunity to practise them. The existing culture of the organisation can be a limiting factor. Another critical factor in selecting external courses is the cost. The better known companies, as you would expect, charge a premium. Indeed staff can be refused permission to attend courses if senior management considers the financial cost to be too high. The purpose of external courses could be one or all of the following:

- To allow delegates to think more clearly and critically about their jobs.
- To understand more about specialist techniques.
- To allow delegates to broaden their experience by seeing how other organisations operate.

Step 4: Evaluation of Training Effectiveness

Some of the reasons why it is important to evaluate training effectiveness are that evaluation enables you to see whether you have met the training needs that were identified; feedback might be gained about the training that could be used for future training; information on the venue and the trainer might prove very useful.

The very act of going to the trouble to evaluate the training is a demonstration of how important you think it is. Evaluation can test that learning has taken place and equally importantly assess the costs/benefits of the training to the organisation.

Training effectiveness can be measured by validation and evaluation. *Validation* is the assessment of whether training has achieved its prescribed objectives. *Internal Validation* assesses whether the training intervention has achieved what it was designed to do. *External Validation* assesses whether the training intervention was based on an accurate identification of training needs.

The intention of *evaluation* is to improve the training provided by assessing which methods are successful. Evaluation is a difficult process. For example by setting an examination at the end of the training period you alter the nature of the training. Several processes in successful training can be distinguished: Hamblin (1974) proposes five distinct levels at which evaluation can take place, and he describes the five levels as being 'links in a chain'.

The reactions level

What did the trainee think about the training? Trainees react to the training by forming opinions and attitudes about the trainer, the method of presentation, their own enjoyment and involvement. Information about the trainees' reactions is relatively easy to ascertain. The trainer can observe and listen to the trainees' reactions. Methods that could be used at this level are rating scales or audits on questions such as presentation, usefulness and level of stimulation. Often the time that these evaluations are sought is immediately after the training period. A good test at this point is 'would you recommend the course to a friend?'

The learning level

Did the trainee learn what was intended? Trainees learn by acquiring knowledge, skills and attitudes. Trainees are capable of translating what they have learned into behaviour within the training environment. Learning is acquired at three levels:

- *Knowledge*: to measure the amount of knowledge, tests could be run at the start and end of the course. The methods for delivering the test could be multiple choice questions, written or oral examinations.
- *Skills*: this can be assessed by practical tests, again at the beginning of training and at the end.
- *Attitudes*: changing attitudes is quite hard to achieve and measure. Well-known methods include brainwashing and indoctrination! One concept of changing attitudes is known as cognitive dissonance. Dissonance theory states that when we have two cognitive inputs out of line (dissonant) it causes psychological discomfort. So, for example, if we believe that university education is a waste of time and money but all those friends we admire most advocate university education for themselves and their children, to relieve the dissonance we have to either change our attitude to university education or change our friends.

The job behaviour level

Did the learning transfer to the job? Trainees can apply the learned changed behaviour back on the job. Some of the techniques that can be used to evaluate learning at this level are:

- Activity sampling/observer diaries. In this technique trainees are observed in order to see whether they are putting the training into use.
- Critical incidents; key incidents are analysed to see whether the new behaviour was present.
- Self-recording, trainees record how they perform certain processes. A test here would be to ask: have the individuals made changes for themself. So, are they now using the PCs on their desks?

The functioning level

Has the training helped departmental performance? The changed job behaviour learnt by the trainee affects the functioning of the organisation and the behaviour of other individuals. The changes may be measured in such terms as improvements in productivity and output or reduction in costs. For large organisations it can be very difficult to evaluate at this level. Has the individual with the PC got everyone else in the department to use theirs?

The ultimate value level

Has the training affected the ultimate well-being of the organisation, for example, in terms of overall profitability or survival? This is the assessment of how the organisation as a whole has benefited from the training in terms of productivity, output or costs. Has our computer literate example got everyone else in the organisation using computers and therefore added to profitability and /or success.

Evaluating learning at the functioning and ultimate value levels share some of the same problems. Measuring the effects of the trainees' job behaviour can be straightforward when a process or system is involved. By changing the system it should be possible to assess increased throughput and output of work. Evaluation of skills such as leadership could be assessed by the number of sick days in the department, or labour turnover. The difficulty is that the changes might be generated by factors other than training. A poor manager may not have any staff leave when there is recession in the economy as there are no other jobs.

Hamblin (1974) states that the levels are 'a chain of cause and effect'. Therefore the chain can be broken at any of its links. For example a trainee may enjoy the training without actually learning anything.

CIRO

Another approach to evaluation is that developed by Rosemary Harrison, a well-known writer on training matters. This approach is the mnemonic CIRO:

Context   – The context within which the learning event has taken place. This will reflect how well the needs were identified in the first place and whether the right learning objectives were therefore set.

Inputs   – The inputs to the learning event, that is, the factors involved in the running of the course. These could be time, money, location, personnel. The cost of all these inputs can be identified to enable an assessment of the effectiveness and efficiency of the programme.

Reactions – What are the reactions to the learning event. Most important will be the learners' reactions but the reactions of other parties involved in or affected by the training will be useful.

Outcomes – The outcomes of the learning event, by reference to the objectives set and the achievement of these objectives. Different levels of outcome could be:
  – outcome for learners,
  – outcomes for the workplace,
  – outcomes for the team/department/unit,
  – outcomes for the organisation.

Having established the importance of the evaluation phase it is useful to look at some typical methods.

Happy sheets

This is the questionnaire offered at the end of many training courses. One training organisation that I am familiar with carefully positions completion of the questionnaires just after the trainer has given out the certificates and thanked everyone for their participation. The intention is that delegates are on a high and are unlikely to say anything detrimental about the course.

Event lifeline

The trainer puts several pieces of flip chart paper on the wall and draws a line horizontally across the paper. The different events of the course are added in chronological order. Delegates are encouraged to comment on the different parts or sessions – positive comments above the line and negative below.

Talking wall

The trainer puts up a series of questions on the wall and encourages delegates to answer the questions on the flip chart or on post-its that can be stuck on the chart. An example of the questions I used on a talking wall recently are:

● What I enjoyed most about this workshop was....................
● The workshop could have been improved by ....
● The workshop should be followed up by ....

The information I gained from the delegates was very clear and will prove invaluable when I run the next workshop.

DEVELOPMENT

Continuing Professional Development (CPD)

CPD has become quite a common concept, it is the idea that members of professional institutes need to keep themselves up to date on new developments in their field. The law profession has been doing it for years, requiring those practising to attend a certain number of conferences or seminars. Likewise the Royal College of Midwives requires midwives who are away from work for extended periods to attend reeducation courses before they can practice again.

CPD is the final stage in the training cycle, it is where we can review what we have learnt and think about its applicability. What that implies is that it requires self-motivation to get involved in our own self-development. Initiatives such as National Vocational Qualifications are very strong on accreditation of prior learning. CPD provides an excellent format to help that process to work.

Management Development

Training exclusively to develop managers is becoming increasingly more popular and pertinent. The idea is to train and develop people in the skills of management. One company in London is doing so much management development it has commissioned a consultant to design a training course that explains to the remaining staff what the principles of management development are, and therefore why its managers are introducing new management practices.

The theory

Training, like management itself, has reflected the theories of management as they have developed. Early training concerned itself with the techniques, skills and knowledge involved in discovering the one best way to manage. Management became a proactive practice primarily concerned with planning, controlling and directing.

After Taylorism and scientific management came Mayo and the introduction of the concept of human relations. That is, the importance of emotional factors. Training reflected this change in that managers were taught how to be participative. Management development became a process of instruction in some core skills such as network analysis and management by objectives and an appropriate attitude to managing staff.

The next development in theory was the contingency approach. This approach is based on the concept that there is no one best way. Managers need to base their managerial strategy on an analysis of their own organisational situation. The emphasis of management development has changed as trainers have now become 'facilitators' of the process and the managers are seen as 'agents' rather than patients. The logical extension of this argument is that training will cease to be a function as ongoing development will become part of every manager's job.

One such initiative that demonstrates this was undertaken by W. H. Smith, a UK retail company, as described by Nixon and Pitts (1991). They set up a management development programme to focus on helping managers to bring about improved organisational performance.

> Instead of assuming that managers have the same needs, learning is linked to overcoming the difficulties or problems identified by each manager, which are slowing progress and development. This approach recognises that each manager has different needs: it puts the managers in charge of their own development; and it offers the key advantage that it is more likely to result in real organisation benefits which can be demonstrated by the managers at the end of the programme. (Nixon and Pitts, 1991)

Management development then is an holistic approach. It seeks to combine emotion and the intellect:

$$\left.\begin{array}{l} \text{Intellect} \\ \\ \text{Emotion} \end{array}\right\} \text{Whole}$$

The practice

The objectives of management development are clearly to increase the overall effectiveness of the organisation. Armstrong (1991) suggests three objectives for management development:

1. Improving the performance of managers. This is achieved by setting and agreeing clear objectives that are easily monitored and assessed.
2. Identifying managers with the potential for further jobs and ensuring they receive the training and development necessary to achieve their potential.
3. Assisting senior management in the task of ensuring that managers are trained and ready to move into higher-level jobs. This may mean ensuring that a succession plan is in existence.

Management development is different from management training because it is more concerned with 'whole person development' and does not concentrate on separately defined skills such as time management or letter writing. An element of management development is that managers need to contribute and want to develop themselves.

Some of the elements of management development programmes have been referred to previously but will be mentioned again here in the context of management development.

Selection. Managers are normally selected to join development programmes and therefore some kind of selection criteria need to operate. Selection could be on seniority, performance, or perceived potential. The methods employed could be testing, assessment centres and appraisal – either of performance or potential.

Education and training courses. Training courses may form a part of the management development process. The options may be in-house courses tutored internally or by consultants or, sending managers on external courses. The most effective will be courses (possibly incorporating internal and external element) designed with the participants in mind.

In the UK business schools are taking a lead in management development. They are either offering open courses or providing consultancy to organisations. The business schools are able to offer a good 'cross-fertilisation' of knowledge amongst candidates. They also offer MBA programmes that can be completely based on the host organisation. Many organisations perceive a link with a business school to be a prerequisite for a successful management development programme.

Coaching. Coaching in the context of management development is where senior managers can help more junior managers to grow and develop their experience through sympathetic coaching.

Mentoring. This approach offers junior managers the opportunity to witness the processes involved higher up the organisation. Mentors will be able to offer advice and help trainees think through their own decisions. It is important that the input from the mentors is non-directive.

Project work. Trainees can be enlisted to work on project teams on matters critical to the business or on work that will provide good experience. An example of the latter might be involvement in community relations.

Secondment. Trainees could be seconded to another part of the business or even to another company. Usually the other company is one that has a good relationship with the organisation and the arrangement is reciprocal.

Competencies

A recent initiative in the UK is 'The Management Charter Initiative'. The intention of the initiative is to encourage management training and development amongst all organisations. The charter offers a 'Certificate of Management' based on certain management competencies. The same defined competencies provide the basis of identification of training needs, self-development and assessment of performance. The Management Charter Initiative would like to see their Certificate of Competence accepted by all organisations as the competencies involved in management will be the same (or similar) in all organisations.

Mintzberg (1973) purports that managers actually spend their lives dealing with many issues per day and on each one they spend little time. They also prefer verbal to written communication. He concludes that managerial activity is too 'complex, changeable and ambiguous' for the measurement of specific competencies.

Outdoor management development

Because management development seeks to balance emotion and intellect it is often practised outdoors – particularly to encourage emotion. After an activity such as an all-night trek across the Brecon Beacons time is spent analysing what happened. The learning points are in the process. These learning points are transferred to leadership, handling conflict or decision making – depending on what the identified training needs are. These outdoor courses normally run on a continuum of voluntarism:

● *Low voluntarism*: a very strong physical profile course. This kind of programme will require outdoor skills. There will be few direct links to the workplace. The emphasis will be strongly on personal development.

- *Medium voluntarism*: some physical skills taught. The emphasis will be more on solving problems and using intellectual skills in an outdoor setting. The emphasis and tasks are more likely to be about teams and work orientation.
- *High voluntarism*: no outdoor skills required. Indeed the setting could be in a high street or on the tube. The emphasis, as with medium voluntarism, will be on intellectual and problem-solving skills.

To help decide what activities will be relevant for an outdoor programme it is useful to relate it to a problem-solving model:

- Problem known, answer known

A problem might be to get an oil drum across a river with only two planks and a rope. The exercise can only be completed successfully in one way, known to the tutor. This kind of exercise is a test of problem solving and intellectual skills and the theory relates quite strongly to problems encountered at work.

- Problem known, answer unknown

The problem might be to move the oil drum over a further distance. There will be a range of options open to the team, none of which are necessarily right or wrong. This level also simulates real life, the company might be suffering in a recession and losing customers. There will be a range of options.

- Problem unknown, answer known

This strategy is not one to be recommended! In terms of contingency theory it is basically unsound because the solution will need to be different for each situation. Unfortunately this is the option used all too often by people who have been successful in the past, it's the 'I didn't get to where I am today without ...' syndrome.

- Problem unknown, answer unknown

This is the *Star Trek* option, boldly going where no one has gone before! The exercise could be to drop people in the middle of nowhere for 48 hours with a map with a pick-up point marked on it. The group will not know what all the problems are going to be. There will also be a range of solutions.

Successful outdoor management development should also comprise 50 per cent activity and 50 per cent review to establish the learning points.

Outdoor management development does come in for some criticism. The main one is that it can discriminate against women. Women are not as physically strong as men and therefore they might only play support parts in very physical activities. Well designed programmes can overcome some of these problems, but if the programme is low on voluntarism and high on physical effort is it really appropriate?

Part III

Good Organisational
Practices

7 Management and Leadership

What distinguishes a leader from a manager? And what is it that makes some people great leaders?

Many managers and writers have searched for the secrets of effective leadership – a search that has occupied a great deal of time and resulted in a large number of words over the years. The reason for the search is the hope that is it possible to define and capture the things that good leaders do so that we lesser beings can reproduce them and be instantly successful.

With a group of students at the University of Surrey I set up an exercise to identify some great leaders. Our list included Hitler, Churchill, Gandhi, Thatcher, Napoleon, Stalin, Genghis Khan and Christ. We then tried to establish any traits common to all. We began with the possibility that they might all be short, but that did not fit everyone. We thought that maybe they had all led their countries in, or into wars, but that did not fit either. We tried to think of other generalisations but found that there were no common personal characteristics.

Perhaps the one thing we can say is that effective leaders act in a way that is contingent upon their environment. Winston Churchill was described as a leader in waiting, waiting for his 'moment'. When his moment was over the postwar voters voted him out. He was perceived as a leader for wartime but not for peacetime. Incidentally, when he was asked how he felt about being ousted by the country he had saved and led through the war years he is reported as saying 'Well, that's democracy, that's what we fought for'.

LEADERSHIP THEORIES

One theorist, Zaleznik (1977), explored the differences between managers and leaders in terms of their attitudes towards work. Some of these differences provide a useful differentiation and can certainly be applied to the leaders listed above.

- Attitudes towards goals: managers are impersonal and passive; Leaders are personal and active.
- Getting things done: managers coordinate and balance in order to compromise conflicting values; leaders, create visions that excite people.
- Relationships with people: managers have a low level of emotional involvement; leaders develop empathy with others.
- Self-perceptions: managers are conservators and regulators of the existing order; leaders work in, but do not belong to the organisation because their sense of identity is not dependent upon the job they do.

So, we have established that a leader has to be appropriate to the situation and the environment (this is obviously a contingency theory view of leadership). Most leadership theories take this as implicit. One theory that provides a good starting point for looking at leadership is the 'action-centred leadership' theory of Squadron Leader John Adair (1979). Adair observed successful leaders in the military context and looked at the functions leaders perform. Action centred leadership is therefore also referred to as a 'functional leadership theory'. Basically Adair identifies three sets of needs that an effective leader has to balance:

- Task needs
- Team needs
- Individual needs

The interrelationship between the needs is portrayed as three interlinking circles (Figure 7.1).

The leader's responsibility is to achieve the task, develop individuals and build the team. Adair describes the leader's responsibilities for each of the different areas. These responsibilities include:

- *Task*:
    - achieve objectives of the work group,
    - define group tasks,
    - planning the work,
    - allocation of resources,
    - organisation of duties and responsibilities,
    - monitoring performance,
    - reviewing progress.

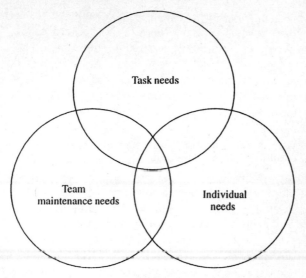

Figure 7.1   Interaction of needs within the group (Adair, 1979)

- *Team*:
  - maintain morale and team spirit,
  - cohesiveness of the group,
  - setting standards and maintaining them,
  - communicating with the group,
  - training the group,
  - appointment of sub-leaders.

- *Individual*:
  - meet the needs of the individual members of the team,
  - attend to personal problems,
  - give praise,
  - reconcile conflicts between the group and individuals,
  - train the individuals.

A second group of leadership theories concentrates more on the dimensions of leadership, that is, the psychological factors. Therefore the style used will depend on the views and opinions of the user. A very influential theory on how leaders can perceive people is the Theory X and Theory Y of Douglas McGregor, which distinguishes between the different assumptions made by managers about human nature.

Theory X is the 'traditional' view that people (workers) are lazy, dislike work and will avoid it where they can. Because of this people have to be coerced and bullied. They need to be controlled, directed and threatened with punishment to make them work. People (generally) do not want responsibility, they lack ambition, want to be directed in their work and just want security.

This theory is very clearly a scientific management approach. The implication is that people need to be shown how to do a repetitive job, rewarded by results they will be happy. This theory is also a self-fulfilling prophecy. If you treat people this way they will almost certainly behave this way. In the language of current management thinking we would call people treated this way 'powerless'.

Theory X is a very influential theory because we see it happening all around us. In my local library recently the librarian in charge was treating the other assistants as complete idiots. She was standing back from the counter and constantly interrupted the assistants to correct them on very minor and insignificant points. She gave them no freedom to act and controlled them absolutely. All this in total disregard of the customers (although local libraries probably do not yet think of book borrowers as customers!)

Another way of thinking of Theory X is to call it, as it was called at one company where I worked, 'mushroom management', that is, you keep people in the dark and intermittently shovel excrement over them!

One of the first recorded uses of these assumptions can be found in the writings of Machiavelli in the fifteenth-century courts of Italy.

It is tempting to say that the class system in Britain perpetuates Theory X. By instilling in an upper class elite an attitude that they are superior, are they not likely – from their positions in industry, commerce and the civil service – to treat workers as people who need to be cajoled, bullied and controlled? Is it the foundation of the paternalistic style of management?

Theory Y is a much more altruistic assumption about people. In this assumption people are seen as workers who like work and find it as natural as rest or play. If workers are committed to the objectives of the organisation they do not have to be coerced and directed. Indeed if the conditions are right people will not only accept responsibility but seek it out. The theory also assumes that people are naturally imaginative and creative and can use these traits to solve problems at work. The intellectual potentialities of the average human being are not being fully utilised.

This Theory Y assumption is much more human relations school – the point for organisations is that they need to operate in ways that encourage individuals to meet their own self-fulfilment needs. Indeed in the 1990s, as recession still grips industry, many companies are using psychological tools to assess managers in great depth. They are doing this because they are aware that promotion opportunities do not exist in 'downsizing' organisations, therefore the organisation wants to uncover other ways of motivating staff and this could be by lateral moves into areas of interest for the manager.

These Theory Y assumptions form the basis of the 'new leadership' movement about which there is more later in this chapter.

The relevance of these two theories to leadership is very clear. Theory X managers will be autocratic and authoritarian and Theory Y managers will be benevolent, participative and democratic.

Most writers on Theory X and Theory Y tell you that the X and Y are extremes and that most managers fall somewhere in between. I am rather doubtful about this – I have seen managers who pride themselves on their toughness and aggressiveness. It seems you have to be one or the other. It is a clear choice of opposites, like the difference between theists and atheists – your position is one or the other.

Leadership Style

A major piece of research in the area of the behaviour of people in leadership positions was undertaken by the Bureau of Business Research at the Ohio State University. This research is known as the 'Ohio State Leadership Studies' and proposes two dimensions of leadership:

- *Initiating structures* is about authority and structure. The leader defines structures and group interaction so that goals can be met. The leader organises the groups activities.
- *Considerateness*: the leader establishes trust, mutual respect and rapport. The leader achieves this by showing concern and consideration for subordinates. This is very much a human relations approach to leadership and reflects the democratic element.

The study found the two factors were uncorrelated. Therefore they create four separate behavioural categories (Figure 7.2).

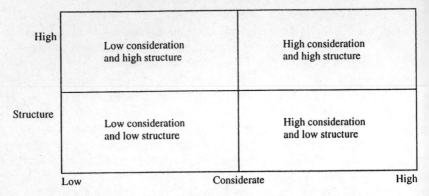

Figure 7.2   The Ohio State quadrants of leadership behaviour

Blake and McCanse (1991) have developed the findings of the Ohio State leadership studies into 'the leadership grid figure' (see opposite). In the grid the various combinations of a concern for people (considerateness) and a concern for production (initiating structures) are characterised by five major leadership styles.

- 9,1   Authority/compliance management: this style emphasises arranging work conditions in such a way that the 'human element' can only interfere to a small degree. An example might be a production line.
- 1,9   Country club management: there is a lot of attention to the needs of people. This is because satisfying relationships are being sought as that will lead to a comfortable, friendly organisational atmosphere.
- 1,1   Impoverished management (or *laissez-faire*): a minimum of effort is extended on getting the work done and sustaining organisation membership.
- 5,5   Middle of the road management: there is a balance between getting the work done and maintaining morale at a satisfactory level. The goal of this kind of organisation is adequate performance. It probably involves relying on 'tried and tested' methods and a minimum of risk taking.
- 9,9   Team management: this approach is characterised by interdependence and a shared commitment to the organisation's purpose. Relationships are based on trust, respect and getting things done by committed employees.

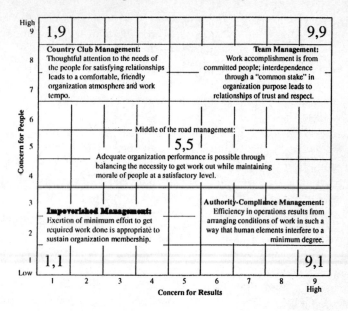

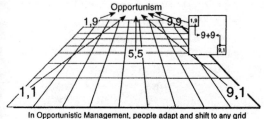

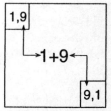

In Opportunistic Management, people adapt and shift to any grid style needed to gain the maximum advantage. Performance occurs according to a system of selfish gain. Effort is given only for an advantage or personal gain.

9+9: Paternalism/Maternalism
Reward and approval are bestowed to people in return for loyalty and obedience; failure to comply leads to punishment.

Source: The Leadership Grid® figure, Paternalism Figure and Opportunism from *Leadership Dilemmas – Grid Solutions*, by Robert R. Blake and Anne Adams McCanse, Houston: Gulf Publishing Company (Grid Figure: p. 29, Paternalism Figure: p. 30, Opportunism Figure: p. 31). Copyright 1991 by Scientific Methods, Inc. Reproduced by permission of the owners.

- 9+9 Paternalistic 'father knows best' management: the leader takes the high 9 level of concern from 9,1 and 1,9 to create a combined style of controlling paternalism. The paternalist strives for high results (high 9 from 9,1) and uses reward and punishment to gain compliance (high 9 from 1,9). The paternalist uses a high level of concern for people to reward for compliance or punish for rejection.
- Opportunistic 'what's in it for me' management: the opportunist uses whatever grid style is needed to obtain selfish interest and self-promotion. They may use 9,1 to push their own goals with one person, and 1,9 to gain trust and confidence with another. Performance occurs according to a system of exchanges.

Having reproduced the Blake and Mouton managerial grid I think it is appropriate to test its validity. With some students I tried to plot some organisations (the assessments were entirely subjective.) We placed Marks & Spencer at 7,7. We thought they were very good to their staff, they seem to look after them well and M&S appear to be a company that people like to work for. They are also very successful and give the impression of being very efficient.

Next we tried to place the British Army. One student, an ex-soldier, wanted to place them at 9,9, but the rest of the group perceived them as more Theory X and therefore around 2 but remaining high on the production axis, giving a position of 9.2. This places the Army in the authority/obedience category.

An interesting observation made by the group is that schools and universities are, due to changes being introduced by the government, moving from an average of about 5,5, which means getting results through a balance of task and maintaining morale (albeit at an adequate level only) to 8,3, which means that concern for results – production (profit) – is increasing and motivation and commitment are slipping. Colleges are being forced to become more concerned with throughput of numbers than with what is actually taught!

The Continuum of Leadership Behaviour

Another major theory in the area of leadership is the work of Tannenbaum and Schmidt (1973), who classified types of leadership behaviour. They proposed that in different situations different leader-

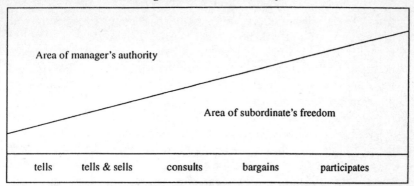

Area of manager's authority

Area of subordinate's freedom

| tells | tells & sells | consults | bargains | participates |

Figure 7.4   A continuum of leadership behaviour (Tannenbaum and Schmidt, 1973)

ship styles will be required and developed the 'continuum of leadership behaviour' (Figure 7.4). Each type of behaviour is related to the degree of authority used by the manager and to the amount of freedom available to their subordinate.

● Tells: the manager makes a decision, announces it and expects staff to carry it out, without question.
● Tells and sells: the manager makes a decision and sells it to the subordinates, perhaps by explaining how the decision was arrived at.
● Consults: the manager presents ideas or tentative decisions to the group for consultation. Having consulted the staff the manager still makes the decision and probably sells it.
● Bargains: the manager outlines the issue and asks for ideas. Informal negotiation takes place until a working compromise emerges.
● Participates: the manager permits subordinates to function within defined limits. The manager and staff together define the issue and arrive at a solution. Theoretically the manager only has as much influence as the others in the work-group.

A development on the idea of the continuum is that there could be a further classification. That is, on the grid to the right of 'participates' could be entered 'abdicates'. Under this classification the manager announces that a problem has been identified and that it must be tackled by the team without the manager's involvement! An example from my experience is that in a previous job I called a meeting with my manager to tell him how much work I had to do and to obtain his help. When I informed him that I had X number of things to do he replied 'You think you've got problems, look at all the things I have to do!' He proceeded to show me his list of 'things to do'. I left in exasperation.

A true contingency theory of leadership is that of Fred Fiedler (1967), 'the contingency theory of leadership effectiveness'. Under this theory group performance is seen as a result of the interaction between the leader and the group and the situation (the structure of the tasks). Leadership behaviour is dependent upon the 'favourability' (situational favourableness) of the situation. Fiedler identified three variables that determine the favourability:

- *Leader–member relations:* how much the leader is trusted and liked by the group members and the willingness of the members to follow the leader.
- *Task structure:* how clearly the tasks are defined and the extent to which they can be carried out by detailed instruction.
- *Position power:* the power the leader has as a result of position in the hierarchy and the amount of authority the leader can exercise over rewards and punishments.

Some conclusions from Fiedler's work are:

1. Appropriate styles of leadership are contingent upon the degree of control present in the various structures.
2. Leadership through influence is likely to be more successful when there is a match between the situation and the style.
3. When there is a mismatch between the situation and the style it is easier to change the situation than attempt to change the style.

So, where does this take us in understanding how organisations work? A particularly important approach is that of Clarke and Pratt (1985). They propose a theory that is situational, depends on the degree of control present and refers to the style being used. They propose that different styles of leadership are required at different stages of an organisation's development (Table 7.1).

Table 7.1 Clarke and Pratt's (1985) contingency theory of leadership

Stage	Style	Description
New	Champion	A champion is required to fight for and defend the business. The champion is a leader who can lead a team with dash and energy.
Growth	Tank commander	A leader who can develop a strong supportive team that is able to exploit the existing market.
Mature	Housekeeper	A leader to ensure efficient and economic management. A leader who is competent at cost-control, planning and using sound personnel policies.
Decline	Lemon-squeezer	A leader who can get the most out of the situation. A leader who is tough and innovative, who can cut costs improve productivity and reduce staffing levels.

So far we have looked at some of the theories behind leadership. The next part of this chapter concentrates on a method for improving leadership skills. This approach, which is called 'new leadership', builds on the work of McGregor and Zaleznik, amongst others, and is an approach used by many successful companies.

NEW LEADERSHIP

Leadership, then, plays an important role in the management of human resources. Both now and in the future successful organisations will be those that can attract the best people, release their energies and talents and use it well. To achieve this organisations need to create and maintain the conditions and the environment within which people can flourish and grow. More and more professional staff (and others) believe that work should be fulfilling, exciting and fun. Work should offer opportunities for learning and growth. Leadership obviously plays a key part in achieving this environment.

Traditionally leadership has been viewed in the following ways (think of Theory X as you read this list):

- The leader is always right and therefore others have little to offer.
- Leaders need to keep separate from those they lead.
- The leader must know all the answers and must not show weakness.
- The leader cannot admit to mistakes.
- The leader is to be blamed if things go wrong.
- People have to be rewarded, threatened or punished in order to perform.
- Leaders often pursue power and empires rather than purpose.

Modern theories state that leadership should be carried out in a way that empowers and respects people. This new leadership requires leaders to (think of Theory Y):

- Develop an inspiring vision based on values and beliefs that appeal to people at every level and encourage them to develop their own vision, and share it.
- Create a climate in which staff can offer their full energy, vision and talents and release their initiative.
- Welcome change and upheaval.
- Make fresh accurate responses to each new situation.
- Give up the pretence that the leader knows best and knows all the answers, accept that the leader is learning also.
- Celebrate success.

One of the points made in the list above, and by Zaleznik (1977), is that leaders need to have a vision of what they want to achieve, what they are striving for.

Vision

This is the skill of having a vision of what the leader is trying to achieve – the idea that in your mind you have a vision of the finished cathedral as you are laying the foundations or mixing the cement. An example of a famous visionary is Martin Luther King, whose personal vision was 'When if not now? Where if not here? Who if not me?'

A vision is intended as a device that provides a picture of a different reality for the future. It is a picture that inspires people to be committed and work hard towards a future objective. A good vision will provide a framework and a sense of purpose. It will identify individual roles and shape commitment and enthusiasm. In essence, then, a vision is a picture of a desired state of affairs. Therefore it is important that it is widely shared and understood.

A good example of a famous vision was that of J.F. Kennedy when he said in the early 1960s that America would have a man on the moon by the end of the decade. His vision excited and inspired people, it set a challenging but achievable target that was realised.

A vision is a passion and therefore it may be best encapsulated by a poem or a quote, or even a symbol, a picture or a piece of music.

A recent example of a powerful vision that I have seen was drawn by a manager in the Benefits Agency. She drew her team going up a steep mountain side. All the team were holding on to each other, apart from two at the bottom of the line. This was to depict two new members of the team. The manager was in the middle, pushing those up ahead and pulling those behind.

Many people like to use music to express their own vision. Some of the most memorable are 'Imagine' by John Lennon, 'Somewhere' from *West Side Story* (particularly the Tom Waits version), 'Chariots of Fire' by Vangelis, 'When you see a chance take it' by Steve Winwood and 'Something inside so strong' by Labi Siffrie. What is your favourite song, picture or poem? What does it say to you?

Mission

A vision can be translated into a mission statement, which provides the organisation, division or department with a target and a way of achieving it. A mission statement is usually produced by the 'top team' in the organisation. It provides:

● A sense of purpose.
● Direction.
● A balance between the business focus and the staff.
● A clear, concise and understandable lead.

The following is a mission statement formulated by a team of which I was a member:

Personnel/Training Team Mission Statement

By working together, in a mutually trusting and respectful environment, we will contribute to the overall success of .... and take the lead in demonstrating the values and behaviours of the Corporate plan.

We will provide professional and enthusiastic Human Resource management by supporting and encouraging individuals to take responsibility and by providing reliable, quality administrative support.

An example of a company-wide mission is the one used by the international division of a major insurance company:

As the leading and largest established commercial Insurer in the UK, our goal is to become accepted as simply

THE BEST

Through the creative use of all our talents, we will build an increasingly successful and profitable business that

- gives the highest quality of service to all our customers
- provides the widest range of competitive products and services to meet their growing needs
- offers challenging, satisfying and rewarding careers to us all.

In so doing, we will have a company in which we can all feel justly proud.

This example illustrates how the values of the company and the aspiration of the staff can be combined to achieve specified results.

Leadership Values

As well as having a mission statement that outlines the values and behaviours you want to encourage, it can be helpful to have a fuller list of the rights and responsibilities of people at work (Table 7.2). The rights relate to individuals and the responsibilities relate to the organisation. The rights and responsibilities are applicable to both management and staff.

Table 7.2   Rights and responsibilities at work

Rights	Responsibilities
To be clear of what is expected of me.	To do what is expected of me.
To get on with my job in my own way once objectives and constraints have been agreed.	To abide by these constraints. To use time productively in achieving these objectives
To have a say/veto in selecting the people who work for me.	To abide by the agreed criteria for selection.
To be consulted about decisions that affect me.	To be assertive in giving my opinions of those decisions and then abiding by the jointly agreed solutions.
To take decisions about matters that affect my area of work.	To communicate them appropriately.

Source: Sue lovegrove.

It is interesting to note that working on rights and responsibilities at work is also an important part of assertiveness training.

Leadership, then, is becoming an important issue, good leadership implies that the company wants to treat its staff well and show respect for them. An important part of this approach is having a vision that can inspire people, as well as releasing their intelligence and initiative. Leadership is not divorced from business itself – it recognises that people are the key organisation's key resource and that therefore people skills are becoming increasingly more important.

8 Performance Management

Performance management is the attempt to get the best results out of a situation. It is an attempt to manage both individuals and the organisation's needs. The chapter finishes by looking at assertiveness, which is a method of getting the best out of individuals.

Performance management aims to achieve better results by understanding and managing performance within an agreed framework of

- Planned goals
- Objectives
- Standards

It is an approach to managing the human resource, using performance. This implies that there is (1) measurement, (2) feedback and (3) motivation. The outcome for the individual is increased commitment and job satisfaction. The outcome for the organisation is increased effectiveness.

Where will we find performance management? It can be found in organisations that think individual development and self-development are important, in organisations that are concerned about finding ways to improve performance. The organisation will need to have a contingency structure because it will need to value flexibility.

A good model of performance management is that of Bevan and Thompson (1991)

- *Objectives and strategy*: the direction could come from a variety of sources. For the public sector, government will set the agenda. In the private sphere the objectives will be generated by the proprietors or the board. It may be that a 'mission' exists or is created to provide the direction. The corporate and business strategies will also yield valuable information.
- *Work performance and motivation*: the objectives and strategy will indicate what the direction of the organisation will be. It will also reveal the actual tasks that need to be completed. Performance appraisal provides a way of managing the tasks and motivating staff to achieve this.

153

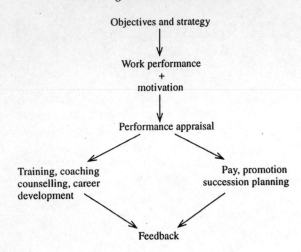

- *Performance appraisal*: appraisal is a technique for getting better results from the organisation, from teams and from individuals. This is achieved through managing performance within an agreed framework of planned goals, objectives and standards.

APPRAISAL SYSTEMS

The implications of appraisal systems are that appraisal:

- is systematic,
- embraces formal and informal,
- provides an integrated systems approach,
- is continuous.

There are normally thought to be three recognised types of appraisal:

- that which assesses potential for the future,
- that which determines reward,
- that which assesses performance.

Potential for the Future

Assessing employees for future potential will usually be carried out as part of a succession planning exercise. Assessing potential is always difficult as it assumes that managers know what skills and competencies are required at the higher level. Also, the usual way for staff to progress is by being good at their present job and – as the 'Peter principle' reminds us – that is not necessarily a good indication of future performance. (The Peter Principle states that successful managers are often promoted to a level at which they are no longer effective, see Peter, 1985.)

Distribution of Reward

Using appraisal as the means of determining reward is a valid exercise. The problem is that the appraisal will cease to have any use as a means of joint problem solving and setting measurable objectives for the next period. Appraisees will be reluctant to admit, or volunteer, any shortcomings if they know that they will be marked 'against them' and therefore possibly lower the potential reward.

Performance Appraisal

There is of course some overlap between these three but for the purposes of performance management, performance appraisal is the system to be used. The objectives underlying performance appraisal are to review performance for the period under review, agree objectives for the coming period and identify training and development needs. A survey conducted by the Institute of Personnel and Development (Hogg, 1988) on 'Why Companies Review Performance', produced the following results:

	Per cent
To assess training and development needs	97
To help improve current performance	97
To review past performance	98
To assess future potential/promotability	71
To assist career planning decisions	75
To set performance objectives	81
To assess increases or new levels of salary	40

Performance appraisal is not the exclusive review system, it is just the formalised one. Managers and supervisors talk to their staff every day – the performance appraisal is an opportunity to take a helicopter view of the situation, that is, to rise above the everyday and look at performance over a longer-term perspective. It provides an opportunity for manager's and their subordinates to understand and agree the standards or performance required.

Benefits to the organisation

The organisation benefits from effective performance appraisal because it reinforces the manager–subordinate relationship. The interview may highlight priorities, problems or successes. Also company-wide training needs may be highlighted as well as individuals with high potential.

Benefits to the manager

Managers benefit from appraisal because they have an opportunity to discuss work, areas of confusion and identify areas requiring coaching or counselling.

Benefits to the employee

The benefit to employees is that they will have a chance to discuss with their manager, their current roles and aspirations for the future (in the present role or another), and agree the performance level required in the coming period.

Objectives of appraisal

If employees are to be promoted, developed and transferred it is important to obtain reliable data to base those decisions upon. Appraisal helps to provide information on actual performance. In the US and Germany it is part of employment law that organisations must run open appraisal systems. Appraisal then reinforces the role of the manager. Effective supervision and planning is a part of a manager's job, as is assessment.

The appraisal system will also reflect the culture of the organisation. Systems can be very assessment-orientated, such as the British Civil Service, which used to operate closed appraisals in all departments. That is, one where an assessment is made of an individual without the employee having the opportunity to question, comment on or even see the assessment. Other organisations run open systems that are much more a joint problem-solving exercise. As with many human resource initiatives appraisal needs to be supported from the top. Senior managers have to appreciate the purposes and ensure that their managers conduct appraisals properly.

The following model describes the different styles that culture or design can give to appraisal:

	3 Tell/sell	4 Joint problem solving
Feedback	1 'Fireside chat'	2 Abdication

Listening

Source: Fiona Ellis.

1. 'Fireside chat': if the style of appraisal is just to give feedback then listening will not be required. When the interview involves little listening and no feedback then nothing is being achieved. The topics under discussion are likely to be peripheral and unimportant.
2. Abdication: if the appraisal is just a matter of listening to the appraisee and giving no feedback or direction then the appraiser is abdicating responsibility.
3. Tell/sell: where the intention of appraisal is to tell appraisees what the appraiser or company thinks about them, then listening is low and feedback is high.
4. Joint problem solving: the optimum box in the model. Both sides are able to talk, listen and give feedback.

The advantages of joint problem solving over tell/sell are as follows:

Joint problem solving style	Tell/sell style
– Purpose is to develop – Appraiser as 'helper' – Appraiser participates in planning and assessing	– Purpose is to evaluate – Purpose is to judge – Purpose is to tell

Appraisal is essentially a communication channel and can be a way to introduce change. It can be used in this way by making the questions used in the paperwork ones that reflect the values you want to introduce. So, for example, you might want to know 'Does this employee perform well with minimum supervision?', rather than question whether managers control their staff properly. Another example might be an excessive pre-occupation with appearance and time-keeping rather than performance.

Appraisal can contribute to motivation. It can contribute by meeting needs, by helping staff to see how they have performed and setting objectives for the future. There will also be a link to reward. In most cases those with excellent appraisals can expect to receive better reviews than those with poor ones.

Lastly, appraisal will provide a means of checking on other systems such as selection. It will be possible to check whether staff are capable of achieving the jobs they were selected for.

Types of Appraisal System

Overall assessment. A manager writes a report, hopefully to some guidelines, on the subordinate. The employee may or may not be allowed to see the assessment and comment upon it.

Grading assessment. This approach is one of the most common in the UK. Managers rate their subordinates' performance against, usually, an extensive list of requirements. Typically they are rated as follows: 'Please circle the performance achieved – Poor/Satisfactory/Good/Outstanding'.

Critical incident technique. This approach looks at key events or incidents in the year or period under review that were outstandingly good or bad. These are analysed to note the critical points. They are then examined by the appraiser and the appraisee and remedies and solutions are sought.

Multiple assessments. Nominated raters complete assessments that are collected and fed back to the appraisee at an interview. The raters could be subordinates, peers or superiors.

Management by objectives. This is the modern approach first described by Peter Drucker (1955). Objectives are agreed and set at the beginning of the review period. Training, development or coaching may be available to assist the employee. At the end of the period performance is reviewed and the new objectives are set. The performance is assessed against quantitative objectives. It is not the personality of the job holder that is being reviewed.

Peer group appraisal. This is the buddy system whereby the members of a small team evaluate each others' performance.

Upward appraisal. This system is the result of the search for a truly objective appraisal system. The basic idea is that people can be judged best by the people who work under them. It is even suggested that upward appraisal leads to better understanding and improved performance. An important part of an upward system is preparing the organisation culture. One of the issues is confidentiality verses openness. Will appraisees give an unfair assessment if the appraisal is private or will vindictive managers look up subordinates afterwards?

Upward appraisal is certainly an enlightened approach and will work in an organisation that has a culture of trust and openness. It will certainly allow staff to feel 'empowered', to feel that what they have to say matters, is important, and is taken seriously.

Douglas McGregor wrote a seminal work on appraisal: 'An Uneasy Look at Performance Appraisal' (1957). He proposed that appraisal has three functions:

1. It provides systematic judgments to support salary reviews, promotion and transfers.
2. It provides a means of informing subordinates about how they are doing, and suggesting changes in behaviour, attitude or skills.
3. It provides a means of coaching and counselling the subordinate.

For appraisal to be effective it must provide good feedback to the subordinate. McGregor identifies this as a problem area because:

1. Managers dislike criticising subordinates.
2. Managers often have inadequate training to handle appraisal interviews properly.
3. Managers often dislike new procedures or methods.
4. Some managers doubt the validity of appraisal.

Other problems identified by McGregor are that managers dislike being in the position of 'playing God' because of an inherent value of respecting people. He also asks whether it is possible to evaluate subordinates like machines in a purely objective way. Another problem is that it can be difficult for managers to relate the needs of individuals' self-appraisal to those of the organisation.

Other criticisms of performance appraisal are:

1. For subordinates to be able to improve performance they need to be given good, accurate and helpful feedback.
2. It is a very time-consuming process. The interviews normally last 45 minutes to one hour. Preparation has to be done, as well as completing the appraisal forms and following up training needs.
3. Appraisals serve the needs of organisations to make judgments about staff without always being of benefit in improving performance.
4. Subjectivity will always be a problem. Managers hold unconscious views on sex, age, race and so on and these form an inherent part of any assessment. This process is often referred to as 'attribution theory'. That is, successful people can be said to be successful because they work hard and are bright, or it can be attributed to being lucky and saying the right things to their bosses.
5. Feedback and follow up is inadequate. If no attempt is made by managers to provide the training or coaching required the system will lose credibility.
6. Poorly designed appraisal forms or irrelevant items will reduce credibility.

7. Managers in different departments or sections will assess people differently. If a normal distribution curve is plotted for different areas in the same organisation the classifications will vary. That is, for example, it will be easier to be rated above average in some departments than others.

8. Managers do not set good enough objectives to review performance against. For example, in one London company an appraisal was found with an objective that read 'to reduce the backlog of invoices'. This objective has no measurable facets. It does not state by when, how or to what standard. Other examples of poor completion of forms were found under a section on training at the same company:

   - X is willing to undertake any further training if necessary to career.
   - Communication training.
   - Management development or team building.

9. The 'halo' or 'horns' effect. It is possible for the appraiser to be excessively influenced by one characteristic only (especially if the characteristic is one the appraisser also exhibits). This can be said in the positive sense to be the 'halo' effect, whereby the appraisee is perceived to be good in all areas. Alternatively one serious fault can lead to the appraisee being marked down in all areas.

So, appraisal can be a subjective scheme but the alternative is rumour and prejudice. A well-structured scheme that is accepted by management and staff is a key tool for performance management.

Performance appraisal can also be criticised on equal opportunities. A recent report by the Institute of Employment Rights (1994) suggested that many schemes were subjective and reinforced sexual stereotypes. The result has been that women have received lower pay rises even when their performance ratings were the same as those of men. This has come about because appraisals are now more common at all levels of organisations and therefore decision making over pay has been pushed down to line managers. The argument is that men and women value attributes differently. Assertiveness, for example, may be considered appropriate behaviour for men but not for women, from whom tact is more highly regarded.

Men were more likely to be offered training and promotion, leading to long-term discrimination. Merit pay also tended to be used as a retention tool in companies with a high staff turnover. Rewarding long servers favours men.

ASSERTIVENESS

A current trend in organisations is to give training in assertiveness. Part of this is due to the fact that organisations are keen to use all the skills and talents of its employees. This may be due to a vision or policy or it may be because organisations that are faced by recession have become very lean. A common word in organisations is 'empowerment'. The concept is about releasing the energy, vision and talents of individuals.

Assertiveness skills help facilitate this by developing communication skills. A lot of assertiveness training looks at the ways we communicate, both verbally and non-verbally. By providing a 'set of tools' that can be used in various situations individuals will benefit from greater confidence as they start to get results from their interactions with others.

Another concept supporting assertiveness is the idea best expressed by Bruce Springsteen (1989) 'If we don't all win, nobody wins.' The idea relates to the concept that the outcomes of interactions with others can vary, so that both sides can finish an interaction by either winning or losing. The outcome for the assertive person is that both sides win. In other interactions either one person or both people lose, and as Bruce says above, if one person wins and one person loses then really nobody has won. This concept can be expressed in a chart:

WIN lose	WIN win
LOSE lose	LOSE win

You

Me

- LOSE/lose: in the work situation you and a colleague cannot agree about how to do something when your manager comes in and orders you both to do it her way!
- WIN/lose: you disagree with your manager about how solve to a problem; eventually your manager tells you that it will be done her way. You have to do it this way but you are not very happy.
- LOSE/win: you want a more junior member of staff in another department to do something for you. You approach the issue by throwing your weight around and telling them what they are going to do. You get a result but lose the respect of the other person (and that person's colleagues).
- WIN/win: you and your boss have different views about how to solve a particular problem. You both discuss the issues and the alternatives. Between you, you arrive at a solution that is better than either of your own individual solutions. You both come away from the meeting feeling good, and with a solution.

So, how is it possible to become more assertive? The first step is to learn to recognise different types of behaviour so that you can respond to them assertively. There are normally said to be four distinct behaviours

- Aggressive
- Indirectly aggressive or manipulative
- Passive (or non-assertive)
- Assertive

Aggressive behaviours are fairly easy to describe. Think of someone at work who is very aggressive and you will see that their behaviour probably includes the following:

- Shouting
- Gesticulating
- Not Listening
- Bullying

- Dominating
- Always being right
- Staring others down
- Invasion of social space*

Indirectly aggressive people probably do not think of themselves as being aggressive, but many of the things they do are very threatening. Their behaviour includes:

- Being uncooperative
- Sarcasm
- Sulking

- Making a fuss
- Huffs and puffs
- 'Looks that kill'

Passive people are ones who watch everything happen. On a course that I ran a few years ago I picked up a phrase from a person who was prone to passivity – the phrase is intended to stop them being so passive: 'this is not a dress rehearsal'. Passive people can be recognised by the following characteristics:

- Unassuming
- Avoid eye contact
- Talk quietly
- Hesitant
- Apologetic
- Avoid excessive body language

- Do not answer back – even when right
- Always say yes
- Lack confidence
- Low self-esteem
- Confused (do not know what they want)
- No boundaries*

Assertive behaviours include:

- Confidence
- Being able to say no
- Smiling more than others
- Do not avoid eye contact

- Open body language
- Persuasive
- Clear objectives
- Do not hog centre stage

*These are references to the idea of social space – the concept that we all have a certain amount of space around us that we like to maintain. With people whom we feel comfortable with we might reduce the space; with strangers we want to maximise it. Aggressive people often deliberately move into our social space. This unconscious (and sometimes conscious) movement is to make us feel threatened, to put us onto the 'back foot' and make us uneasy. The suggestion here (no boundaries) is that passive people find it hard to maintain their individual social space, and because they do not give out any body language signals of intending to defend it, it is invaded by other people!

Advantages and Disadvantages of the Types of Behavior

Why do people behave in these ways? After all even the most passive person must see that there is some advantage in behaving in a passive way, and that's why they do it.

Aggressive. Aggressive people do, I believe, think they are getting results. Unfortunately they attain results at the expense of the other person. Aggressive people certainly get themselves a hearing and gain their own way, however they achieve this in a way that shows no respect for others. The disadvantage of aggressive behaviour is that enemies are formed. The phrase that springs to mind is 'those that live by the sword, die by the sword.'

Aggressive people become narrow minded because they do not listen to other people, but continue behaving in the same way, becoming even more unapproachable. Their interactions tend to be WIN/lose.

Indirectly aggressive. I think indirectly aggressive people feel superior to other people and they tend to be rather self-centred. They can therefore be devious and cunning. By keeping their distance they are able to maintain for themselves the idea that they are superior. These people can also, then, be rather two-faced. It must be very tiring knowing that you are right all the time!

Because indirectly aggressive people are not being honest with themselves or with others their interactions will predominantly be LOSE/lose.

Passive. I am convinced that passive people act passively in the belief that it will lead to a 'quiet life'. They think that by being passive they will avoid conflict and that people will like them. The reality is that they are perceived as people who have no respect for themselves, as people with no 'get up and go', and people who do not get what they want. Passive people LOSE so that others can win.

Assertive. Assertive people are confident people, and because they are confident they know what they want and therefore they get it! As they know what they want, they get more satisfaction from the work they do, because they are doing work that they want to do. The only real disadvantage of assertive behaviour is that others might not recognise that you are being assertive and think you are being aggressive. Also, other people might be envious or jealous of your success. Assertive people ensure the outcome is WIN/win.

Verbal Indicators

What are some of the things that these people typically say? The following list is to enable you to be able to spot the behaviours in others (and yourself!)

Aggressive:
'You will'
'I want'
'Do this'

Passive:
'Yes'
'When you've got a minute'

Indirectly aggressive or manipulative:
'If you do this for me ...'
'You're the best person for the job'
'You're the only one I can trust'

Assertive:
'Together ...'
'Mary, I would like us to ...'
'Tom, thank you for your help'

Non-Verbal Skills

Assertiveness training also looks at the non-verbal skills used in each of the behaviours as an additional way of recognising them.

	Aggressive	*Passive*	*Assertive*
Voice	loud	quiet	expressive
	harsh edge	whisper	
	overbearing		
Speech patterns	direct	tongue-tied	pauses for
	talk fast	stuttering	others to
		slow	speak
		embarrassed	
Facial expressions	staring	worried	relaxed
	unresponsive	covers face	smiles
		blank	
Eye contact	stares	none	keeps eye contact
	'boring in'		(listening with
			their eyes)
Body movement	invasive	steps back	open
	smothering	inconspicuous	relaxed
	intimidating	sits at back of	
		room	

Behavioural Blocks

One of the critical features of understanding assertiveness is to understand what the individual behavioural blocks are that stop us behaving assertively in certain situations. In many ways work on assertiveness is about 'self-development', it is about, as is counselling, understanding what makes us tick. Much assertiveness training has to skip over this whole area – and that is probably justifiable – as commencing to analyse our personal patterns requires intensive one-to-one work and takes some time! Think about stereotypes of the neurotic American as played by Woody Allen, who joke about going to their therapists every week for years.

So, what are some of the typical behavioural blocks? From the workshops I run on assertiveness I have begun to make a list.

Upbringing

This is clearly the place to start. Sociologists state that the first five years of a child's life are the most critical or formative years. In these years we learn the behaviours that will be with us for the rest of our lives. For myself, I know that one of my 'patterns' is a problem with authority. Looking back, when I worked full-time in organisations I did not really get on with the boss I had at any one time. My expectation of bosses was always very different from what they delivered. I always, I think, expected too much from them. Indeed I had thought for many years that I would like to work on my own and be my own boss, and this is what I have ended up doing. Anyway, my point is that the relationships I had with my bosses was formed by the relationship I had with my parents as a young child.

My parents had a clear set of values that they wanted themselves and their children to live by. These values were imposed on me and I was not given a chance to question them – I was not allowed to question their authority. Therefore, on the one hand I was expecting my bosses to tell me what to do (and be right), and on the other hand I did not want to be told what to do.

I do not think the issues described here are very different from the experiences of many people growing up in the 1960s. Indeed the swing towards questioning the values of the time were a feature of the 1960s and the early 1970s with TV shows such as *Monty Python*.

So, to finish off a very drawn out example, I personally do not like being told what to do by anyone and I think the reason for this is that when I was a child the culture was a very proscriptive one. That is, parents and teachers knew best and were not to be questioned. An example of this culture is that I am naturally left-handed but when I was at junior school in the mid-1960s I was made to write right-handed because that was the way that children were supposed to write! Children were not allowed to experiment and learn by discovery. The frightening thing is that the hand you write with, or your leading hand, is decided genetically and there is nothing we can do to change it!

Personal rights

As individuals we have the right to be heard, listened to and taken seriously. I think that sometimes people forget they have these rights, particularly when they are in new situations or with people they perceive to be more important than them. If you think back to the section on power, the point about power is not that other people have innate power but that we attribute them as having power over us.

Another complication is that we often disregard our rights. So, for example, a perfectionist can find it very hard to admit mistakes in themselves. Clearly we all make mistakes but we punish ourselves for failings that are unavoidable and inevitable.

One of the techniques that is used to remind people of what their personal rights are is to write out a 'bill of rights'. This can include:

- The right to be treated with respect.
- The right to be listened to and taken seriously without fear of retribution.
- The right to say no to unreasonable requests.
- The right to make mistakes.
- The right to choose not to assert oneself.
- The right to work in a safe and healthy environment.
- The right to be treated on equal terms as human beings.
- The right to be treated as an individual.
- The right to privacy.

What is important is that we all formulate our own bill of rights, including the things that are most relevant for us. The bill of rights can also be very useful for people who are passive and want to become more assertive. The bill of rights will provide a framework for their decisions.

Not knowing what we want

This I think is the curse of passive people. They are not really clear about what they want out of life, therefore in each situation they are not clear what the right course of action is. Aggressive people do not have this problem because the options they take always revolve around their being the centre of attention, or about meeting their needs.

One of the influential concepts in management and training at the present time is the concept of 'empowerment' (see Chapter 11). A large number of people, both within and without organisations have been made to feel powerless. This is a debilitating state that saps energy, therefore management 'gurus' are looking at ways to empower people in organisations. Tom Peters sums up the change required for managers in his book *In Search of Excellence*, cowritten with Robert Waterman (1982). Leaders in organisations need to change from:

- Managers   to leaders
- Cop   to coach
- Referee   to nurturer of champions
- Devil's advocate to cheerleader

One strategy for all people is to think about a range of responses to opportunities. So, if we sell our house we work out the minimum amount we need to recoup, have an idea of how much we think it is worth and an idea of how much we really want. Therefore we have three positions:

- Ideal position: sell house for £100000 and make reasonable profit.
- Realistic position: sell house for £95000. It should move quickly and yield a small profit.
- Fallback position: sell house for £92000. This will pay off the mortgage and give the minimum profit to pay the costs of moving.

If we take the house example, it seems to me that many people find it hard to sell their house because they have not considered the realistic position and are not aware of their fallback position.

How will this strategy work in the work place? The boss approaches you at 4.55 pm and tells you that an urgent report is required for tomorrow and you have to do it. You have arranged to take your partner out for a birthday drink. The passive person may go straight to the fallback position and say 'yes'. The assertive person will consider the ideal position, which is to do the report tomorrow, and the realistic position, which is to do an hour on the report tonight and the rest first thing in the morning, negotiating from a position of strength. Aggressive individuals would not have been asked, if they had they might have given a two-word response!

Logic

One delegate on a course explained that his problem was logic. He was a graduate in computer sciences and now worked in a computer department. All his tasks relied on logic, except his dealings with other people. He had a background of shielding his emotions and now found it difficult to express them to get what he wanted. This issue is very important as I think that assertiveness has a lot to do with explaining your feelings to people as a way of being heard and expressing what is important to you.

Assumptions

Another delegate had a problem in that she was a secretary working for several directors, one of whom told her what to do all the time and gave her no freedom to act. The secretary was very bright and clearly had a lot that she could contribute and this was recognised by some of her superiors. The assumptions arise around the attitude of the boss who insisted on treating her as a junior, or as a child. The secretary also had her own assumptions regarding how secretaries are supposed to act and telling the boss how the situation could be a WIN/win was not one of the duties of a secretary! (Refer back to Transactional Analysis in Chapter 2 for another interpretation of this situation.)

The Self-Fulfilling Prophecy

Another concept that is particularly relevant to assertiveness is the idea of the self-fulfilling prophecy. To see how it works let us begin with the passive person. Passive people believe that their views are not very important so they behave in a very meek and mild way. Other people see them behaving in this way and assume that they do not have anything to contribute so they are treated as if their views are unimportant. The message passive people receive is that other people do not value their opinions and this reinforces the idea that they do not have anything to contribute. If we think back to the 4 Boxes model, passive people are always heading for a Lose box.

Assertive people are clear about what they think and act as if they have something important to contribute. Other people can see that they are prepared to stand up for their right to be heard so they treat them with respect. Assertive people see that others respect what they have to say and this gives them the confidence to say it.

Assertiveness opens a door for organisations to change. It allows the organisation to work on change at the individual level and empower people. For more on change see Chapter 10.

Being Assertive

What do you need to say to be assertive? After you have recognised the desire to want to treat people with respect and to gain WIN/win outcomes you will need to use the language of assertiveness.

Use 'I' not 'you'.   Using 'I' is very powerful, it involves saying what is right for you. Assertive people also refer to others by their first name as a way of reinforcing that they are on the same level.

Be direct and brief.   Do not waffle or say too much. Make your request clearly and concisely.

Say what you want or how you feel.   Feelings again. By saying how you feel about something you are making a statement that no one can take away from you. Facts and opinions can be right or wrong but your feelings are yours and can not be taken away from you.

Listen.   Aggressive people cannot do this because they see no value in what anybody else has to say. Assertive people can listen to other people's views, opinions and feelings – and respond accordingly.

Starting to be assertive.   What is important is to start with some easy targets. Try shops or restaurants and build up your confidence and courage. Go for small victories first before taking on your managing director. One last key thought is that you have the right not to assert yourself. If you consider it is likely you will come off worst in an encounter by trying to be assertive (particularly against experienced aggressors), then you have the right not to assert yourself – as long as you have considered the options.

9 Counselling and Coaching

This chapter will concentrate on the two key management skills of counselling and coaching.

COUNSELLING

Counselling is a key skill for leaders and managers. It focuses especially on feelings. Feelings can block rational decision making and personal growth. They may be generated by incidents at work or at home. These feelings dissipate our energy as, for example, we have a need to understand the direction of our career, or as we struggle with financial problems. Counselling is also a key tool for managing change. Counselling allows individuals to work through and come to terms with changes, whether for good or ill.

Solving people problems should form a part of every manager's job. A manager will not hesitate to respond to problems arising with the work, but is often very uneasy with problems of a personal nature. There may be many reasons for this. The most likely is that for many (male) managers getting involved in 'emotional' issues is something they have had no 'life-experience' of. Their socialisation has made them suppress their emotions and not talk about them. Leading on from this, many managers think that this is the sort of work that the 'touchy, touchy, feely, feely' lot down in personnel should be dealing with. A third reason may be that managers have had no training in how to deal with 'personal problems' A further reason is that many managers, particularly senior ones, have no one they can turn to. In these days of 'empowerment' (see Chapter 11), managers who are reluctant to take on a counselling role may be perceived by their staff as having a lack of concern for them as people.

The British Association of Counselling defines counselling as 'helping people to help themselves'. A way of interpreting this is to see counselling as a means of helping individuals with personal problems. A personal problem that overwhelms one person may be a mere irritation to another, but the problem is a 'gap'. Counselling helps to bridge the 'gap' between the current situation and the desired one. Often problems are more felt or imagined than real, but if they are felt to be a problem then they are a problem.

There are many reasons why helping employees is good management and employment practice. Stress related illness accounts for a large percentage of the days lost through illness in this country and others. A counselling culture will help to reduce the number of days lost. Some organisations may wish to be, and wish to be seen to be, caring employers – counselling can enhance the image. It may be that the organisation has caused the stress in its employees by overworking them, introducing change or relocating them. Therefore the organisation has a responsibility to help them.

Vaughan (1976) quotes three themes on counselling:

1. Counselling is a person-to-person form of communication marked by the development of a subtle emotional understanding, often called 'empathy'.
2. It is centred upon one or more problems of the client.
3. It is free from authoritarian judgements and coercive pressures by the counsellor.

Some of the advantages of using counselling are:

● It is a process that helps people deal realistically with actual and/or imagined problems that are reducing performance or a sense of well-being.
● It can be preventative in that it can be a way of alleviating or preventing stress.
● It can help clients to identify feelings, emotions or misconceptions that prevent them from understanding their situation realistically.
● It enables clients to make appropriate choices between strategies.

Different approaches to counselling exist and the approaches of the key schools of thought are:

● *Psychoanalytical*: concentrates on past history and the internal dynamics of the 'psyche'.

- *Client-centred*: Non-directive counselling. The approach places more faith in and gives more responsibility to the client in problem solving.
- *Behavioural*: applies principles of learning to the resolution of specific behaviour.
- *Cognitive*: a belief that people's problems are created by how they conceptualise their world. Change the concepts and the feelings will change too.
- *Affective (gestalt)*: this is the gestalt approach. Pain and distress accumulate and have to be discharged before the individual can become 'whole' again.

A continuum of counselling styles, can then, be seen. The two extremes are directive and non-directive counselling:

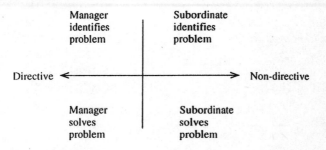

Perhaps the seminal work on the subject is Gerald Egan's book *The Skilled Helper*. Egan's approach is person-centred rather than problem-centred. It is often only after trust has been established that clients will discuss what is really bothering them. The good helper respects clients for themselves and not for the problems they bring.

The model for *non-directive counselling* is as follows:

Helper skills required	Tasks for the client
(1) *Pre-helping phase* – the helper must attend to the client, both physically and psychologically, and 'be for' the client.	
(2) *Phase 1:*	
(a) Responding (to the clients frame of reference)	To explore their own behaviour
(b) Empathy Concreteness Respect Genuineness	To examine their problem
Phase 2:	
(a) Stimulating (the client to alternative forms of reference)	To seek action oriented self- understanding
(b) Advanced empathy Self-disclosure Confrontation Immediacy	To own the consequences of self-exploration
Phase 3 (helping to act): Suggest new directions Behavioural support Action programmes	To act on their understanding

Non-directive counselling operates by clients reaching their own decisions. Counsellors establish a relationship of trust by empathy and being authentic. They can give relevant information about their credibility and react honestly. Counsellors do not impose their own opinions, their task is to facilitate their clients' own abilities and strengths so that they can experience the satisfaction of having defined and solved their own problems. Counsellors can provide additional information on points of fact or in situations where the client is incapable of generating alternative strategies.

The two phases of non-directive counselling are:

Phase 1: Establish rapport: Reduce anxiety, listen, show empathy, show respect, increase the client's self-confidence, be 'for' the client.

Phase 2: Explore the situation: see world through client's eyes, explore underlying problems, reflect, clarify and summarise, sensitively confront – if necessary, explore alternative solutions, allow client to select best solution, agree on realistic action plan.

Individual, Self-Developmental Counselling

What we have looked at so far has been an approach to helping people with real or imagined problems. An advance on this is to use counselling as a way of keeping in good shape. So, for people who have no real problems it is a way of helping them to discharge some of the feelings they have accumulated about things that have happened to them. In effect we are talking about a *proactive* approach to change. Counselling in this sense can help us to work on situations of change and upheaval. The counselling may help to put us 'in touch' with why we are finding certain changes difficult to cope with.

The theory behind this different use of counselling is based on the premises of McGregor's Theory Y (McGregor, 1960), that is, people are basically imaginative and creative, they are 'zestful' and full of energy and fun. They are also intelligent creative and loving. If you ascribe to the Theory X view that people are basically lazy, indolent and need to be bullied to do anything then developmental counselling is going to be difficult to effect.

McGregor goes on to say that the reason we all too often behave in a Theory X way is because that is the way we are treated. There are countless examples of where people are treated well and listened to, and perform at a much higher level. Often what stops us behaving in the Theory Y way is the 'distress' we pick up in our lives. The distress is the emotional side of us coming to the fore. We often have distress patterns that are rigid ways of responding that we developed as children. When under stress at work some people are unable to let other people help them, they feel they have to do everything themselves.

Another (all too common) pattern is about rejection. Some people feel they have to push relationships as far as they can to test whether the other person is a real friend or will reject them. When they have pushed the other person too far they are rejected and it reinforces their self-fulfilling prophecy that they are useless and unlovable.

The purpose of counselling is to identify the distress pattern and therefore discharge the distress. Unfortunately this can be the painful part. Discharging distress can take many natural forms. I see my three year old daughter discharging hers by crying, screaming, shaking, sweating and expressing anger. Her distress can be discharged very quickly and five minutes later it is forgotten. For adults it is not so easy, we pick up messages that a lot of behaviours are socially unacceptable for adults – this makes it difficult to discharge the distress.

One of the best things that has happened to me as an adult is learning to cry again – crying is one of the things that men in our culture are definitely encouraged not to do. However, I think there is hope for all men from that unlikely source, the footballer Paul Gascoigne. In the 1990 World Cup finals Gazza was visibly crying when the emotion of the situation got to him. (He had been booked for a second time and if England had qualified for the final he would not have been allowed to play.) It was encouraging to see a large public figure openly crying, and the fact that it was understood and not frowned on was important. Crying is certainly a good and comprehensive way of discharging emotion, but whatever the method it is important that individuals get the distress out in a healthy way.

This approach to developmental counselling is best achieved by finding someone you like and trust and both of you agreeing to help each other. You may want to meet once a week and agree to spend 15 minutes each being the counsellor and the counsellee. The process and content is the same as normal counselling. This kind of regular counselling can help to put the pieces of your life into some kind of sense. I like to think of it as completing a jigsaw. We may not quite know what the whole picture is, or even the size of the finished jigsaw, but the insights we gain can start the jigsaw in one corner and gradually help us to move across.

Let me give you an example of how this process can work. Recently, at a regular counselling session, I raised a topic that had been bothering me. I had been experiencing emotional problems when building towers with my 3-year-old's wooden bricks. That is, I understood that the fun for a 3-year-old is knocking the tower over but I was getting quite upset if she tried to knock it over before I had finished building it. So what, I hear you say! Well, normally I am quite relaxed but what was coming out was some of the stress of being self-employed, of having to be in control of everything and doing things my way. Not startling revelations but it helped me at that time to put things into perspective.

The following section reproduces an article I wrote for the Surrey European Management School's summer 1993 newsletter. I think it captures quite clearly the importance of counselling as a management tool, and also the significance of an individual's emotions in a changed situation.

Counselling: An approach for Improving Management Performance by Managing Feelings

A couple of years ago, when I was a personnel manager for a company in London, I was told by the personnel director that the office was closing. Everyone was to be offered either a new job or redundancy. I was determined to make sure all the staff would get the best possible advice and every penny they deserved. One evening, after a couple of months, I arrived at Waterloo Station in plenty of time to take the 6.24 as usual. However there was no sign of the train and nothing on the information screens. I was incensed, I went and found a British Rail employee and in a very aggressive way explained my dissatisfaction with the cancellation and BR generally. I was literally shaking with anger and wanted to punch the poor chap.

A couple of days later I reflected on my behaviour, it seemed strange that I was so 'wound up'. Usually people describe me as easy-going. Looking back now I can see that I was discharging nervous energy or emotion. The stress of making people redundant had built up inside me and needed a release. Unfortunately for the poor BR employee he was my focus of release.

It is interesting to note, although we are slipping off at a tangent here, that BR staff are used to having people 'discharge' at them. They therefore act in a very detached way to their customers so that they do not have to take the comments personally. This detached behaviour, however, seems to work as a self-fulfilling prophecy and encourages people to 'discharge' at them.

This discharge of emotion is carried out by everybody. Some of the common ways of achieving it (or attempting to achieve it) are by metaphorically 'kicking the cat', having a large drink, or two, playing sport, or doing something completely different such as gardening or painting tin soldiers.

In my example of a changed situation, the office relocation or redundancy, I propose that what we did wrong was to take no account of emotion when planning the redundancles. As well as making sure that all the practical things were being done properly and taken care of, we should have looked after the emotional side of the staff affected.

Change and its impact on individuals is, I think, the biggest cause of personal problems. A recent book by Makin, Cooper and Cox (1991) proposes that human beings do not like uncertainty.They propose that most people form instant impressions of others – even if that first impression is later proved wrong. It is easier to reduce the tension – brought about by the uncertainty – by forming an impression and then changing our opinion later.

Humans, then, do not like change and uncertainty because it produces tension and stress. It also means that the attitudes and behaviours we hold are questioned. This attack on our attitudes and behaviours is called cognitive dissonance. An example could be of moving house. In the first week it is likely that you will have real doubts about whether you have done the right thing. The new house is bigger but it needs decorating, all your friends have been left behind and no one seems friendly in the new road.

What is happening is that all the doubts about the new situation need to be weighed up against the supposed pluses of the old – we go through a process of changing our attitudes. For example, where before we rated accessibility to a public house as high, we now have small children and want to live in a quiet road near a good school.

Throughout our lives, and increasingly at a faster pace, we are in changing situations. The changes in our situation and our attitudes produce stress and emotion that needs to be discharged. So what are some of these feelings that are aroused? There may be guilt about what we have done, or even not done. There may be fear and uncertainty about the unknown, or even fear of the known. Self-doubt and feelings of inadequacy might arise. There may also be grief about saying goodbye to some things or people, or anger at having to make LOSE/lose decisions.

What then can be done to help ourselves and other people cope with their feelings in a positive way? The age old solution is what in personnel terms is called 'tea and sympathy'. I think this is a reflection of the fact that people often want to talk about their problems (a problem shared etcetera) or to discharge their distress. What personnel and line managers need to do now is to learn some skills to help their staff to manage stress and the feelings they generate. The best approach to achieving this is to use non-directive counselling.

A definition of non-directive counselling is that it is a way of helping people help themselves. As the name implies, the aim of non-directive counselling is to help individual clients (those being counselled) to solve their own problems. The counsellor is there to help the client by listening, by listening in a non-judgemental, respectful way (this skill is a lot harder that it sounds!) The counsellor has to be someone who respects the clients and wants to help them solve their problems or understand why they are feeling so angry or desperate. One way of thinking of the relationship is that the counsellor is there to assist clients to solve their own problems through their own abilities and strengths. The counsellor helps them to achieve the satisfaction of defining and solving their own problems.

Learning counselling skills is not easy but it will provide managers with a skill that will help their own development and provide an approach for getting the best out of their staff. British Rail staff might appreciate it as well!

If you are interested in more information on counselling some writers and speakers to look out for are Bruce Nixon, Gerald Egan, M. Reddy, Michael Megranahan, Robert de Board and Martin J. West.

COACHING

Coaching is a tool for managers and leaders to improve task performance. This is achieved by leaders maximising the output of their staff. Megginson and Boydell (1984) give the following definition:

> Coaching is a process in which a manager, through direct discussion and guided activity, helps a colleague to learn to solve a problem, or to do a task, better than would otherwise have been the case.

Effective coaching needs thought and preparation, as well as some skills. Managers need to be clear about the outcomes they are trying to achieve and flexible about when to coach. Setting fixed times for coaching is one option, relying on critical incidents is another.

Megginson and Boydell propose that four key features influence coaching as a strategy:

- The formal learning system: that is, the systems and procedures formally in place to identify training and learning needs.
- Other learning opportunities: acquiring skills and experience while in the organisation.
- The learner: the learner has to be receptive to the learning opportunities available.
- The learning climate: do the values, beliefs and culture of the organisation support risk-taking, the occasional mistake and a collaborative atmosphere?

Coaching should be informal and part of the normal process of management. Effective coaching will help subordinates to be aware of how well they are performing. Incidents or new work will be used as opportunities to coach and teach new skills. Coaching can also be used to tackle projects or one-off assignments.

Coaching may come across as informal but it needs to be planned. Effective coaching is a motivational tool that will develop and stretch employees. The following skills (presented in Megginson and Boydell, 1984) are useful in the coaching situation and can be used in a wide variety of other situations. Any individuals who master all these skills will find that they start to achieve more from their interactions with other people.

- Attentiveness: if the coach is really going to help people attention must be paid to them. Attentiveness also shows respect and honesty and helps individuals to feel they are being taken seriously.
- Paraphrasing: the listener repeats back what the speaker has been saying. The purpose of this is to establish whether the listener really has understood what was being said. It also shows that the listener was listening and attending. It is clearly a good practice to seek clarification of what the other person is saying. It is easier to rectify mistakes at the beginning of the process rather than later.

- Recognising and expressing feelings: as we have already seen, feelings are very important and can often be a barrier to people expressing themselves clearly. The requirement is for the coach to show empathy with the other person. By being aware that the other person is having difficulty the coach can respond accordingly.
- Suspending judgement: this skill is the counselling skill of 'being for' the other person. Coaches need to suspend their own judgement so that they can help others to address their problems in a way that is appropriate for them.
- Silence: for many people silence is uncomfortable but it is a key skill for getting the other person to talk. Most people feel uncomfortable during silences in conversations. If the coach is leading the conversation silence should be used to make the other person respond.
- Giving and receiving feedback: this is really a very difficult area and can produce the wrong results when handled badly. What is important is to make sure that the feedback the coach gives is specific and is given in terms of the coach's reaction to the behaviour.

Part IV

Making the Ideal Organisation

10 Change and Organisation Development

Change is a factor of everyday life in our modern world. Change is present within society as a whole and within the organisational context. Successful companies need to develop strategies to ameliorate the effects of reacting to change. This is achieved by developing a pro-active approach.

Introducing change effectively is a key management skill:

> There is nothing more difficult to take in hand, more perilous to conduct or more uncertain in its success than to take the lead in the introduction of a new order of things. Because the innovator has far more enemies in all those who have done well under the old conditions and only lukewarm defenders in those who might do well under the new. (Machiavelli in *The Prince*)

CHANGE

Change is a permanent feature of our existence. For example the 1990s have produced far greater competition. The opening of the European Market has removed barriers between EU countries. The computer has revolutionised many areas. In the workplace computers have replaced many clerical jobs, and on the shop floor automated, robot controlled car production is the norm. Social changes occur also. The 'baby boomers', who used to wear 'tightly fitting' Levis, are now into middle age. Their physique has changed shape with the years and they now require 'loose fit' jeans. Levis have introduced jeans to accommodate this change.

Values

A good way of capturing change is to look at values. Values held in society change over time. The following list is my interpretation of changing values.

Old values:	*New values*:
Efficiency	Enterprise
Production	Marketing
Conformity	Initiative
Authority	Leadership
Achievement	Self-actualisation
Self-control	Self-expression
Independence	Interdependence
Endurance of distress	Capacity for joy

Some of these changes have been evolving since the Second World War; some seem to have been accelerated by the Thatcher years of the 1980s.

The change from authority to leadership has been gradual. At one time a person wearing a uniform (police, headmaster) was automatically shown respect, but now respect and trust have to be earned. Some of these changing values encourage individual development and recognise the importance of that.

A good example of a change in values is that reflected in the Green movement. Concern for the environment and over-dependence on non-renewable resources have become major issues in the developed countries, with eco-summits taking place. Ten years ago the population as a whole knew little about the ozone layer. Now supermarkets are selling 'environmentally friendly' products that are more expensive than 'environmentally unfriendly' ones but sell very well! Where once a Green vote was a protest vote it is now a deliberate vote for a way of life.

Paradigms

The values of our society, or our own subset of society, can also be observed in the paradigms we adopt. Paradigms are the 'mind sets' we develop, the particular way we have of looking at society or our surroundings. We looked at the collapse of the British motorbike industry in an earlier chapter but we can now revisit it. One of the failings of the industry was that it did not see Japanese competitors as a threat. The paradigms of the people in charge were that the public wanted large-capacity bikes; that buyers would continue to 'buy British', whatever; and that Japanese quality was inferior.

Paradigms can therefore be deep-seated beliefs, or even prejudices, that are very hard to overturn. A part of good management development and organisational development training is input on paradigms, or problem solving and decision making to help managers overcome entrenched 'mind sets'. One description of the objective of this type of training is provided by the comedian Ben Elton. He calls it the 'Pot Noodle idea'. Pot Noodle was a brand new product that did not detract from any existing products. That is, it did not make an existing product obsolete. It was a genuinely new idea or concept.

I heard what was probably an apocryphal story about the search for new ideas. A hundred years ago an American manufacturer of sandpaper was going through a bad time (perhaps we could say that the sandpaper manufacturer was going through a rough patch?) and was likely to go bust. The managing director called everyone together and said he was offering $100 for the idea that would save the company. Two weeks later he called everyone together again and asked for their ideas. Only one person broke the ensuing silence, saying sandpaper could be used for shaving. He said that it had made his face a bit sore but after a week his skin had started to harden up a bit. The boss was pleased with the effort and gave the man $50 but decided the idea was unusable. However the same man came back a couple of weeks later and said that he had been sanding some wood in the garden when it started to rain. He noticed that before the sandpaper fell apart, when it was slightly wet, it did a better job. The boss liked this idea and 'wet and dry' sandpaper guaranteed the future success of the company.

There are three levels at which organisation change can be recognised and managed see Porter *et al.* (1975):

- The individual
- Groups and teams
- The whole organisation

Change and the Individual

One option is to change the individual – to sack those employees who are resistant to change. It is useful, though, to explore the reasons why staff may be resistant to change. Kotter, Schlesinger and Sathe (1986) propose four reasons for resistance to change. We shall look at these in some depth. They propose that the resistance is based on history, on what has happened in similar situations in the past.

Self-interest

Individuals perceive that changes will affect their jobs and their range of power and influence. If their analysis is that the change will be detrimental to them they may try to block it. We looked at types of power in Chapter two but the lessons are the same in this instance. If individuals think that their range of influence will be diminished in some way they may well be resistant. In the past organisation change may have affected their jobs in a way they did not like.

Lack of trust

This is probably down to poor communication. When those affected by change have not had the changes explained to them, or where in the past changes have not brought the results promised, the trusting relationship becomes tainted. Participation would produce better results.

One of the lessons from the Hawthorne experiments in the early 1930s was the 'participation hypothesis'. This stated that significant changes in human behaviour can only be brought about if those who are expected to change are able to participate in deciding what those changes will be.

Many organisations spend a lot of time and energy developing working relations, particularly in teams, so that trust can be established within the team. The reasoning behind this is that the group will work better together and achieve better results. An exercise carried out during outdoor training provides an obvious example: teams have to develop trust, physical and intellectual, in order to achieve the result of all crossing the river with one rope, an oil drum and a kitchen table!

Different viewpoints of the benefits

Different views on the need for change, the actual changes and the outcomes produce different perspectives. Somehow the attitude persists that all change is good. A good example is to think of the world: one perspective is that the source of the world's overall poverty was the switch from agriculture to industrialisation; a different perspective is that progress leads to an improvement in the quality of life.

If you watch politicians on the TV programme *Question Time* or in parliamentary broadcasts they have very different interpretations of how to solve problems and about what course of action to follow. Neither side is necessarily right or wrong, just coming at the problem from a different perspective.

Low tolerance for change

Psychometric assessment tools all have a section for how well individuals cope with change. The evidence is that some people are poorly equipped to cope with change while others are always happy to try new ideas and ways of doing things. Does this take us back to the nature versus nurture argument?

It is obvious from the above four points that one of the key issues in change is emotion, or rather how individuals feel about the proposed change. Change in an organisation will have an effect on values held and therefore the practices and behaviours required. Individuals need to be helped through the process of change. Change means that people's attitudes and behaviours are being challenged. This can result in strongly held feelings, feelings such as:

- Guilt, about what we have done or not done.
- Fear, of the unknown (or known).
- Self-doubt, about how we will cope.
- Inadequacy.
- Grief about saying goodbye to established ways or people.
- Anger, at 'having' to take certain actions.

All these negative feelings produce distress. This distress often causes inappropriate responses. As discussed earlier, a good place to see inappropriate responses is at the ticket barriers of the major London train termini. When trains are cancelled, delayed and so on (as so often occurs), normal, sensible people can be seen behaving very aggressively to British Rail personnel. Ticket collectors are not (directly) responsible for the cancellation of trains, but commuters lambast them aggressively. The commuters are exhibiting untypical behaviour and 'discharging' the distress and stress that has been accumulating. They are showing misdirected aggression.

Coping with distress, releasing our feelings is, I think, something we learn not to do. Children are always able to respond at a feelings level – if they do not like something they generally cry! What we are seeing is the proof of McGregor's Theory Y. People are naturally expressive and enthusiastic but this is bred out of them.

Another emotional response to change is that people can experience the five stages of grief. One of the companies I work for is relocating to the Canary Wharf development in the reclaimed Docklands east of London, and I have seen the staff going through these five stages:

- *Denial*: at first people said that it could not happen, it was just an elaborate joke.
- *Anger*: people then started to say that it was just not acceptable, they would rather leave than go to Docklands. There were a lot of raised voices.
- *Rationalisation*: 'I suppose it makes sense for all the divisions to be together on one site. Although there will be job losses it should make the company more effective and efficient.'
- *Acceptance*: staff started to take advantage of the offer of a half day off to go and look at the site.
- *Renewed action*: when the plans came round for the new building staff started to negotiate for more space and looked at ways to make their function more efficient.

The only problem with this example is the company did not manage the process very well. When the plans were circulated one department of four people noticed that there were only desks and chairs for two in the new building. When this minor point was raised two of the team were informed that they were being made redundant! All staff are now looking very carefully at the plans. Indeed one department of six has chairs and tables for ten on the plan. This is causing great anxiety.

What can happen with the stages of grief is that people can move up and down quite quickly. Some little piece of news, such as raising the canteen prices at the new site, can move everyone back to indignant anger.

The five stages can also be used to analyse personal grief. Take the breakup of a relationship:

- *Denial*: it's not true that she's left me. I'll wake up in a minute. She'll come back tomorrow.
- *Anger*: if I see her or her boyfriend I'll run them over! (Actually a friend of mine did have an ex-girlfriend drive her car at him.) Other approaches are to cut the crotch out of all his suits and to give away all the wine in the wine cellar.
- *Rationalisation*: all we did was argue anyway; she never put the lid on the toothpaste; he never really liked my friends, and so on.
- *Acceptance*: well it has really happened, maybe next time I'll find the right one.
- *Renewed action*: I'm going to get my disco gear down from the loft, join a dating agency and start living again.

These examples show that change as a process needs to be managed at the individual level. The best method to help individuals cope with change is counselling. RELATE (Marriage Guidance Council), Alcoholics Anonymous and psychoanalysis (amongst others) all rely on counselling to help individuals cope with change. (Refer back to the Hawthorne Investigations for more background information on the value, and effects of counselling, and Chapter 9 for a more detailed interpretation.)

Change and Teams

Elton Mayo (Roethlisberger and Dickson, 1939) identified in the Hawthorne studies that team building is an effective tool for overcoming problems brought about by change. Teams can have an important part to play in the change process – those that are pro-change can influence others. Current thinking on introducing change incorporates identifying a network of managers who are receptive to change and developing them. The fear of the group members is likely to be that their interests will be broken up or that the interests of the group will be threatened. This might be relative to other groups internally or externally to the organisation. Refer to Chapter 2 on teams for a more detailed interpretation

Change and the Organisation

Organisation culture and organisation change are clearly linked. The culture of the organisation will determine how easy it is to introduce change and how successful it will be. Organisations such as the Post Office developed in a way that a set of rules and procedure was available for every situation. As new or different problems arose new rules were added. It ended up with a very large manual! And it still did not hold all the answers. These organisations have an efficient solution to yesterday's problems but find it difficult to react to current problems.

Some of the reasons why organisations resist change are:

● Cost/risk
● Return on investment
● Lack of confidence
● Lack of skills
● Potential failure
● No perceived need
● Lack of knowledge
● Time

This list is also a good list of reasons why organisations *should* bring about change.

I think the above list can be condensed into two key reasons:

● *Investment*: change is expensive. Establishing a manufacturing plant that is highly automated in an area where the skills required are to be found is an expensive option for an organisation with an existing factory and workforce in an unfavourable area.
● *Threat to power or influence*: as well as groups within the organisation undergoing readjustment, relations with other organisations can change. The internal readjustments can cause a great deal of pain and grief, and power struggles can be bloody battles at the top of the organisation.

ORGANISATION DEVELOPMENT

'Organisation development' is the generic term that embraces the different approaches to dealing with organisation change. Basically organisation development, as Beckhard (1969) proposed, 'must be planned, must be organisation wide, must be managed from the top'.

It is a strategy, then, that leads to an improvement in the organisation's overall effectiveness. It is an approach that leaves the organisation as one that deliberately promotes and plans change. Part of the process involves developing the capacity and capabilities of the employees and the opportunities for them to contribute to the goals of the organisation. It is then a planned and integrated approach to change that considers the organisation as a whole.

Organisation development has four stages: diagnosis, intervention, maintenance and review.

Diagnosis

The first step is a detailed analysis of the *current situation*. Valid data can be collected by appraisal or surveys. The mission and objectives of the organisation will need to be examined and an understanding of the culture and values of the organisation developed. The systems and processes will also need to be understood.

The problems, resources and opportunities available should all be analysed to produce a *preferred situation*. The next step is to develop the aims and methods to achieve the *desired situation*. Both long- and short-term plans will be required.

Intervention

Intervention can take different forms. A good example to follow is that advocated by Schein (1969). He proposes that the organisation development consultant (whether internal or external) should assist the organisation in its analyses, planning and implementing by helping the process to function rather than by providing the analyses or conclusions. The idea is that the process consultant helps to enable the organisation to solve its own problems. The consultant can withdraw once the organisation is committed to its course of action and has learned the skills necessary to overcoming further problems.

Some of the interventions that can be used are:

● Attitude surveys
● Sensitivity training

- Team building
- Supervisory style training
- Leadership training
- Developing problem solving expertise
- Vision building
- Coaching and counselling

Organisation development intervention can incorporate some or all of these techniques. It is essential to involve line management in the implementation and to make the change permanent. Human resource management policies need to be integrated into the strategic plan, which will need to be achieved with employee commitment and be flexible.

Maintenance

The maintenance element is ensuring that the organisation and its staff are able to cope with further change and that the intervention is not a one-off event. Approaches that can be used are:

- *Behavioural modelling*: demonstrating the ideal behaviour and asking individuals to model it. As they get better at modelling the desired behaviour it will be positively reinforced. Modelling is, though, rather skin deep and the behaviour being modelled may not be a good example to start with.
- *Transactional analysis*: this is the idea that we have to be confident about ourselves and our abilities before we can behave decently and courteously to others (see Chapter 2).
- *Staff involvement*: regular fixed meetings can be organised for all staff in a department to look at work processes and work out ways of improving them. This is the basic idea of 'quality circles'. Problems can arise when all the problems have been solved. There is nothing left to say.
- *Compensation and incentives*: similar in approach to behavioural modelling but rewards are given to those that exhibit the required behaviour.
- *Job evaluation*: one of the new ways of operating will be an acceptance of the importance of individual effort. Performance will be better monitored and therefore the question of internal relativities becomes of prime importance. To ensure the differentials are right a review of job evaluation may need to be established.

● *Differentiation and integration*: Lawrence and Lorsch (1967) propose that successful organisations will need to manage differentiation. As the skills required in the organisation become more diverse (differentiated) it is necessary to manage the integration to keep all the parts together.

Review

The success of the changes will need to be assessed to check whether the desired outcomes have come about. According to systems theory it is likely that change in one part of the organisation will lead to change in another part, so probably the best action plan is a rolling one. To be successful change needs to be introduced with plenty of warning. This is achieved by giving lots of information and allowing participation in the decision making. (See Table 10.1 overleaf.)

Case Study

Organisation change does not have to be a dramatic all-or-nothing revolution. It can be a carefully planned evolution. The following case study is based on change at a residential home for the elderly. I am indebted to Sharon Hadlow of The Princess Christian Homes for allowing me an insight into how she runs the home. This case study will demonstrate:

● The difference between proactive and reactive change.
● The link between change and organisation culture.
● The effect of change in the environment.
● Planning change at the individual, group and organisational levels.
● Minimising resistance to change.
● The importance of communication.
● The importance of participation in the decision making process.

The home that Sharon runs is part of a group that caters for ex-servicemen. The culture in the past has always been one of functionality and organisation based on military standards.

The need for change has arisen due to the increased competition provided by other care homes. Also, the clients have higher expectations, perhaps generated by higher expectations in society generally. What they are trying to change is the culture and practices of the home.

Table 10.1   Pym (1986) personality characteristics and performance in organisation change

Less successful	More successful
Orientation	
Towards equilibrium	Towards growth and change
Concern for safety and security	Risk taking
	Desire for new experiences
Sentiments:	
Preoccupation with means	Greater attention to ends
Belief in 'one best way'	Openness to more than one strategy
Work aspirations	
Regularity and order	Responsibility
Financial security	Achievement and challenge
Prestige and status	Interesting work
View of technical skills:	
Boss is the expert on the	Boss no longer needs to be the
subordinate's job	expert
Leadership:	
Efficiency and human relations	Efficiency and Human
are separate features of behaviour.	Relations are merged.
Submissive	Authority according to contribution
Directive and authoritative	Equality
Decision making:	
Adoption of previously	New approach based on
successful solutions	systematic evaluation of the evidence

One of the changes was the introduction of new dining arrangements, with table cloths and place settings. The reasons for this were to enhance the dining facility, to improve the standards for the residents by improving the quality, and as a longer term objective to make the facilities appear more attractive to potential residents and local authorities. The catalyst for change in the world of residential care was the Community Care Act (1990). This allowed for greater competition in the marketplace.

Change in any setting can be very uncomfortable and disruptive. It can cause instability and uncertainty. Change in a residential home for the elderly can have a devastating effect on people who are perhaps already vulnerable. Change has to be managed very sensitively.

An analysis of the potential change at the organisational level revealed the following considerations:

- *Cost*: the financial cost was found to be manageable when taking stocks into account. It was decided to purchase settings gradually to reduce strain on planned financial resources.
- *Additional workload*: introducing table cloths and place settings would add to the existing workload for staff by adding to the laying, relaying, cleaning and laundering time taken. A quantitative job evaluation was conducted and it was found that it was feasible to incorporate the new duties within the existing posts.
- *Possible resistance*: resistance was possible from both the clients and staff. To minimise the possible resistance extensive consultation was introduced. Both groups approved of the change but preferred a gradual introduction and a trial period. So, all interested parties were involved in the decision-making process and were able to feel a sense of ownership of the decision.
- *Method and plan of implementation*: after the consultation process it was possible to purchase the necessary equipment and set a date in January 1994 for the change to take place.

Place settings are now fully introduced and have proved to be very popular with everyone.

This apparently simple change of introducing tablecloths can be seen to be of supreme importance to the people it affects, both staff and residents. It also confirms the ideas of systems theorists, and particularly the socio-technical systems theory of Trist (1963). That is, change in one part of the organisation or system will have an effect on some other part of the organisation or system. We can hopefully minimise the effects of the 'other' effect by taking a proactive approach to change.

QUALITY

The idea of quality was first introduced by Dr W. Edwards Deming in the 1940s in America. America chose to ignore his thinking and instead the Japanese adopted many of his ideas as they reconstructed after the Second World War. In the 1980s America rediscovered quality.

Quality is putting excellence into practice. For manufacturing, quality is the target of zero defects. There is an apocryphal story that British Telecom ordered 10000 telephones from Panasonic and to comply with their European suppliers they stated that the minimum default of the goods was 5 per cent (that is, they expected 5 per cent of the telephones to be faulty as they would expect from a European supplier). Panasonic therefore only sent them 9500 as they knew all their telephones were supplied with no defects.

One of the current experts on quality is Phil Crosby (1978). He developed a 14-point programme for introducing and managing 'total quality management'.

1. Management commitment: the top management have to be really committed to the idea of quality.
2. Quality improvement teams: teams have to be established to look at the procedures of the organisation.
3. Quality measurement: outputs have to measured and recorded so that changes can be seen.
4. The cost of quality: the cost of doing things badly and the cost of doing things well have to recorded and compared.
5. Quality awareness: everybody has to be made aware of what the quality objectives are.
6. Corrective action: systems need to be established so that improvements to existing systems can be introduced easily.
7. Zero defects planning: zero defects is the idea that nothing is done incorrectly. Existing systems need to be analysed to make sure that they are not building defects in.
8. Supervisor training: training is a very important part of ensuring quality. It is therefore vital that those leading others are well trained.
9. Zero defects day: when the quality of the existing systems has been improved it is possible to plan for a day when there are no defects.
10. Goal setting: goals and objectives need to be set to ensure there is continuous improvement.
11. Error-cause removal: effort has to be put into ensuring that errors do not arise in the future.

12. Recognition: it is vital to give recognition to staff who make a real effort to ensure high quality. Many hotels now tell you who the employee of the month is.
13. Quality councils: committees or councils of staff can be established to look at ways of making their workplace more efficient.
14. Do it over again! The ethos of quality is one of continually striving for improvement.

In the UK the British Standards Authority specifies for suppliers and manufacturers what is required of a quality system. The standard is BS5750. It provides a format for a total quality management approach, a continuous process that requires:

● Measurement of quality.
● Measurement of the cost of quality.
● Incorporation of quality objectives into strategic plans.
● The total quality management approach to be built into the accountabilities of every job.
● Quality teams to be established.
● Training to be part of the process.
● Quality improvement to be recognised and rewarded.

Quality introduces into an organisation many features of good management. The problem is that some organisations would like to introduce only some of the items that improve quality – quality is a system and therefore all the elements need to be incorporated. The other criticism of quality is that it is a very mechanistic process and is therefore most suitable for stable mechanistic environments such as factories and production. Recently organisations such as accountancy practices have also achieved the British Standard.

CUSTOMER CARE

An alternative to total quality management is customer care, which relies on the 'attitudes' of the service provider being caring ones. Customer care programmes concentrate on the level of service provided by the organisation and are therefore most applicable to service companies. Like total quality management, customer care involves attaining excellence but the process is quite different. Whereas the former

involves procedures and systems, customer care involves changing attitudes and behaviours. Customer service generates feelings; very good
or very bad service makes us feel either good or bad. As human beings
we are basically hedonists and like to reexperience the good feelings
but not the bad ones.

So, to change an organisation in to one that provides quality service
means changing attitudes and behaviour. Traditionally organisations
have operated as pyramidal structures:

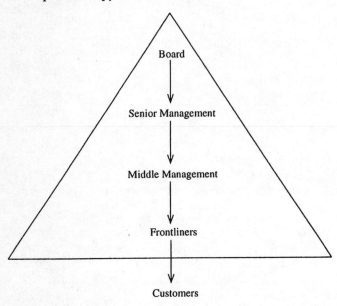

In this model policy and decisions are formulated at the top and
then passed down the organisation. This is a formal one-way model
that is slow moving and discourages dynamism and initiative. An
approach to customer care exhibited by such organisations is that
those at the top send down an instruction, say, that all telephones
must be answered by the third ring. They may use their authority to
ensure this happens, but the actual conversation is the 'moment of
truth' and they have done nothing to ensure that the conversation is
excellent.

Jan Carlzon (1978), the president of SAS airways, worked out that
SAS carried 10 million passengers a year. To make his company

successful he wanted every one of those 10 million to fly with the airline again. He worked out that each passenger interacted with five members of staff, whether the pilot or the check-in clerk. This gave 50 million 'moments of truth' that needed to be managed when a passenger met a member of staff. If on any flight a passenger had a bad experience with one member of staff the good work of the other four could be obliterated.

Current thinking is that the customer is the most important person and the organisation exists to serve the customer. The role of the board and senior management is to ensure that the frontliners, the people who carry out the customer interaction, have everything they need to ensure that the interaction is successful:

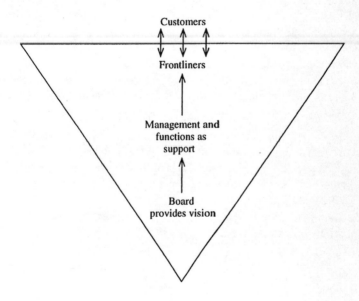

In *A Passion for Excellence* Peters and Austin (1987) describe how organisations create and sustain a competitive edge. They list five factors.

1. The 1000 per cent factor. Jan Carlzon took over SAS airways and turned the company around, using only existing resources. He repainted and reequipped the airplanes, provided new uniforms and trained the staff in customer care. He said 'We did not seek to be 1000% better at anything; we sought to be 1% better at a thousand things'.

2. Customers. Peters and Austin quote examples, but basically they are saying that the customer is the most important person. They advocate some steps for putting the customer first:

- Naïve listening
- Staying in touch
- Measuring customer satisfaction

3. Innovation. Sustainable strategic advantage can be gained by innovation. Peters and Austin identify three key features:

- *Speed* (later the subject of a book by Peters): speed is becoming more and more important in providing a competitive edge – speed needs to lead to reliability.
- *Champions*: product champions who are committed to the product. Charismatic people who can make things happen.
- *Bureaucracy*: organisations need a culture and structure where people can innovate, try things and get involved in things they care about.

4. People. People are the key to excellent customer service. They need to be encouraged to show commitment and ownership of the duties they are responsible for. The authors propose 'reciprocal altruism' – the notion that if we are nice to other people they will be nice to us!

5. Leadership. The key to excellence is a leadership that can tie all the previous points together and add value. The changes are:

- Manager   to leader
- Cop   to coach
- Referee   to nurturer of champions
- Devil's advocate to cheerleader.

They state that leaders should show enthusiasm and pride.

Putting Customer Care into Practice

Customer care is worth consideration by all organisations, after all 'You don't have to be ill to get better!' Customer care can be an organisation change exercise, indeed limited effort and lack of direction will produce minor or ephemeral change only.

Hopson and Scally (1991) propose a twelve-step formula to success.

Step 1: decide your core business. In *In Search of Excellence* Peters and Waterman talk about 'sticking to your knitting'. The idea is that you have to know what business you are in. For example Porsche cars offer status and style first and a motor car second. The car is good but other cars are cheaper, faster and so on. What Porsche are selling is a badge. One that says something about expense and success. Porsche have recognised this and they advertise in a way that is selling a lifestyle.

Step 2: know your customers. This step requires an organisation to find out and understand what customers want so that you can offer them a little more than they expect.

Step 3: create your vision. Sir John Garnet, former chairman of the Industrial Society, a management charity, used to tell a story of when he visited a tractor factory. He walked down the assembly line and asked a man what he was doing. The man replied that he was putting nuts on bolts. When Sir John asked the same question of the next man he replied that he was helping to feed the Third World. That is an example of how a vision has been transferred to staff that they can associate with and believe in.

Step 4: define your moments of truth. Jan Carlzon took this phrase from the bull-fighting arena in Spain. It describes the moment of decision for the bull and the matador. For us this means defining and managing the critical moments of customer contact.

Step 5: give good service to one another. The basic premise is that if staff are not treated well themselves they may become cynical about being expected to treat customers well. So, service standards need to be modelled on internal customers. Hopson and Scally propose that the organisation can help to assist the development of good internal relationships by designing a positive, creative, exciting environment. They also advocate training and more training.

Step 6: Manage the customers' experience.   The skills that need to be developed are: making people feel special; managing the first four and last two minutes; demonstrating a positive attitude; communicating clear messages; showing high energy; working well under pressure.

Step 7: profit from complaints.   Organisations should have in place a system to elicit and deal with complaints. Statistics show that most dissatisfied customers do not complain so it is important to get your customers to tell you what they think. Systems could be established to unearth complaints. Such systems could be telephone surveys, questionnaires or staff surveys.

Step 8: stay close to your customer.   The implication is that managers should stay close to their staff and keep them informed in the same way as customers should be kept informed. Some of the techniques for keeping close to the customer are: maintain a dialogue with them; keep them informed; issue newsletters and magazines; have senior people on the frontline; create partnerships with your customers.

Step 9: design and market the service programme.   This is a key step in putting the initiative into action. Some of the steps will involve selecting and training the customer care champions, designing and running training for all staff, establishing communication channels and letting the customers know what you are doing.

Step 10: set service criteria.   The nature of the jobs in the organisation have to be changed to reflect the importance of customer care. So, job descriptions have to be rewritten to incorporate it, the appraisal system has to reflect the new values required and rewards have to reflect the behaviours you require. The criteria required do not need to be imposed. The most successful will be those agreed jointly with the staff.

Step 11: reward and celebrate service success.   Methods of reward need not be financial. Other methods are badges, trophies, awards, gifts or use of company facilities. At Selfridges in London, service quality is detected by management, customer comments and bogus shoppers, hired by the company. Excellent staff are awarded bottles of champagne at high profile ceremonies conducted by senior managers.

Step 12: develop the service programme. To make service initiatives work there has to be top level support. Setting up a working party or standing committee will be required in order to monitor and steer the initiative. A twelve-step programme such as this should be developed and followed.

11 Empowerment

The purpose of empowerment is to free someone from rigorous control by instructions and orders and give them freedom to take responsibility for their own ideas and actions, to release hidden resources which would otherwise remain inaccessible (Jan Carlzon, 1978).

When managers are truly empowered, the burden of proof should be on head office to tell them why they can't, rather than on them to prove why they should (Valerie Stewart, 1990).

The subject of empowerment has been deliberately left to the end of the book because empowerment is an approach that brings together many of the strands and ideas examined earlier. Many people look for a 'Weltanschauung' or philosophy of life to live by. Ten years ago 'quality' was going to be the guiding principle but it never delivered as much as it offered. Empowerment can offer an approach to organisations that will enable them to succeed *and* treat themselves, their staff and their customers well.

I believe that empowerment offers a way of treating people with respect and honesty, which must be the sign of a civilised society. It offers a modus operandi for organisations that want to be successful in the climate of constant change in which we now live. Empowerment offers a way of dealing with situations where we do not yet know the questions. It provides organisations with an approach that will help them find some possible answers.

WHAT IS EMPOWERMENT?

Empowerment is the concept of giving people more responsibility for how they do their own job. It is about more involvement in decision making and being encouraged to investigate their ideas fully. Empowerment is a process to increase efficiency and make greater use of each individual's contribution. It implies synergy – the whole can be greater than the sum of the parts. Empowerment can be broken down into three distinct areas:

1. Ownership
2. Teams and leaders
3. Culture and structure

Ownership

Empowerment is about ownership. It is a way of involving people in the operations of the organisation, such that they feel personal responsibility for their actions. If people feel that they own their actions or decisions for the organisation then better action will be taken.

The traditional conservative (and even Conservative) view of organisations is the 'stockholder' model: the organisation is in existence to make a profit for the shareholders (or stockholders). and the staff and pensioners are further down the line:

If the objective of the organisation is solely to make a profit then it can engage in ecologically unsound practices; or if the management believes that it will lead to profit, Theory X management is practiced. With this approach no other factors need to be taken into account.

One view is that this is the policy of the Conservative Party, for example privatisation is an approach that comforms with the stockholder model. The privatised water companies have been offering huge rewards to their managing directors based on the financial returns they have generated for their stockholders. The political perspective could be: is that the best way to assess their performance when sewage is being washed up on our beaches and water is being wasted because of old or leaky piping? Is this the approach that culminated in

'Thatcher's Britain' of the late 1980s and was captured so brilliantly by Neil Kinnock as the 'me, me, now, now, I, I' society?

The 'stakeholder' model is a different approach, one that seems much more pertinent to the 1990s and beyond. It is an approach that takes into account the external environment and interacts with it. The model in its basic form looks like this:

- *Employees*: the employees achieve reward and recognition, and both staff and management have an input in decision making.
- *Community*: The organisation has a commitment to the local community in terms of job opportunities and disposable income. It may provide facilities for outside use (such as sports grounds). At the macro community level there is a responsibility to be environmentally aware. This may be in terms of pollution or in building aesthetically pleasing offices.
- *Customers*: the customers are looking for reliability and value for money. They are also concerned with the wider implications, for example there is a campaign to boycott the goods of a certain Swiss-based confectionery manufacturer that is pushing the use of its powdered baby milk in the Third World. The campaign is based on the idea that the company is doing this to make a fat profit rather than acting in the interests of mothers and babies.

Another example of this syndrome is the 'Buy British' mentality. Some people will deliberately buy British goods if there is a choice. Of course what they do not realise is that Europe and the rest of the world are now so intertwined that investment in the company could have come from outside Britain. The electricity used to power the process is by coal imported from Eastern Europe and burned at a British power station. Other raw materials used in the process are imported from Africa and ready-assembled sub-components have been manufactured and completed in Taiwan.

- *Pensioners*: those with an interest in the success of the organisation such as pensioners and subcontractors are involved and kept informed.
- *Shareholders*: the organisation still needs to perpetuate itself, there needs to be a return on investment but what is also important in the financial marketplace is confidence and a positive image.

Perhaps the stakeholder view can best be summarised by a Christian Aid Week campaign that had the slogan 'Mutually responsible and interdependent'. This provides a good summary of the stakeholder view and of empowerment itself.

Teams and Leaders

Successfully empowered organisations are based on teams that are working well and cooperatively. We have already seen that a lot of work on organisation change concentrates on teams. This is because they are the building blocks of organisations.

Some of the activities that will need to be developed can include multiskilling, or in other words learning each other's jobs. The advantages of this is that it teaches staff additional skills and provides the organisation with greater flexibility. Staff can be moved around in times of crisis to do other work. In Japanese companies, where lifetime employment is guaranteed, staff will expect to do whatever the organisation requires them to do. By giving staff more skills their ability to do their jobs and their satisfaction levels can both be raised.

A second important area for teams is encouraging them to contribute ideas on work methods. This process may be achieved through systems such as quality circles or regular, formalised meetings. The team may be encouraged to agree amongst themselves how the work should best be organised and distributed to achieve team targets and organisational goals. Bonus or performance pay schemes may be introduced that reward the team rather than the individual.

The whole approach requires managers to lead their people and get the most out of them. Organisations need to operate as inverted pyramids. Refer back to the second of the models presented in the section on customer care in Chapter 12: the frontline workforce are the face of the organisation – they are the ones who interact with the customers. The role of management is to manage that process and ensure that it works successfully. The board is the fulcrum upon which the organisation can change direction.

So, managers are leaders, a resource, and need to lead in a way that encourages empowerment. They will need to act in strong participation and involvement mode. The job of empowered managers is becoming harder. In slimmer teams they will have to manage poor performers and either train them or move them out. There is no room for slack. The other members of the team deserve to be protected. Also, leaders will have to manage the appraisal process better. If staff are to left to 'get on with it' then the 'it' needs to be very carefully agreed and worked out. How will managers measure performance and how often? There is no longer room to fudge the issues.

The other skills that new leaders will need are staff development, counselling and coaching. Staff development is covered in Chapters 6, 7 and 8, counselling is covered in Chapter 9.

One of the outcomes of empowerment for individuals and teams will be that jobs will become more interesting as individuals will have more responsibility and the opportunity to influence events. This will lead to increased motivation for the individual and improved morale for the team.

Structure and Culture

The organisation will need a culture that is open and responsive to change. The Japanese word *kaizen* means continuous improvement. When you learn a new skill you can make tremendous improvements in the early days but as you grow more proficient the improvement becomes smaller and smaller. There is a danger of thinking that no further improvement is possible. However top athletes break records by 100ths or even 1000ths of seconds. If they did not believe that they could improve by even these small amounts, or believe that it was worth it, they would not be able to go on.

For culture change to happen there has to be a clear commitment from senior management and the involvement and participation of all staff. Management will need to change from issuing directives and acting in the way of the traditional hierarchical pyramid, where the board at the top provides direction to the tiers of managers, staff and users below. I received a lovely example of the unempowered organisation when I rang one of my clients at 12.35 pm. The telephonist put me through but there was no answer. The telephonist then informed me that they must have gone to lunch in the department I wanted. I foolishly asked her if she could take a message for me. Her reply was: 'I'm sorry, I'm not allowed to.'

The new way will be to provide the overall direction and vision, and then set targets, questions and challenges. The implication for the structure of the organisation is that it will become flatter as management layers are reduced due to staff taking on more responsiblity. When Michael Edwardes took over the troubled British Leyland in the 1970s the first thing he did was to remove several layers of middle management.

EMPOWERMENT AND TRAINING

A key change process in creating and maintaining an empowerment culture will be training and development. Training needs to use top management to help them work through and plan the changes required. Training can facilitate their 'visioning'. Another key area is the training of management. They are bound to experience a lot of uncertainty and fear about whether they will keep jobs. Some managers will have to adopt a whole new way of managing their staff. Finally the staff will need influencing and assertiveness skills. After years of being told what to do they will need help to change their approach. Assertiveness training is a good way of changing attitudes. Some degree of communication skills will be useful too so that the empowered staff can communicate with each other. One of the outcomes of empowerment is there will be lots of staff on the same level who will be required to interact with each other. Influencing and assertiveness skills can help to make these exchanges more successful.

EVALUATING EMPOWERMENT

How will you know that the empowerment exercise has been worthwhile? Some of the obvious ways of checking the success of the programme will be by random interviews at different levels to see how jobs have changed. Do the jobholders have more responsibility; are their departments being more successful? There may be statistical evidence to show increased performance, decreased costs and even decreased sick absence – all indicators of staff motivation.

Another well-used method would be to conduct an attitude survey. This could be done both before and after the changes to gain information on general satisfaction or involvement in decision making.

EMPOWERMENT IN ACTION

In this section we are going to look at a case study of empowerment in action as well as at an example of a training workshop that could be introduced to enhance or develop the empowerment process.

Case Study

The subject of this case study is Harvester Restaurants, a division of Forte. In particular the Dulwich restaurant is featured. (The details of the case study are taken from an article by Jane Pickard published in *Personnel Management* magazine in November 1993.)

The Harvester empowerment plan was highly structured and linked to delayering. Because of this it was seen as highly threatening by many staff. The structure now is that a branch manager works with a 'coach', who handles all training and some personnel issues. Everyone else is a team member of some description.

In the first six months after empowerment was introduced staff turnover rose as those who did not want to change left. Many people lost status – one employee who had been taken on as an assistant manager became a waitress. However, as she had some special skills she became a 'team expert' (having mastered special responsibilities or 'accountabilities' one becomes an expert). A team can be entirely made up of experts, and experts are elected by the team.

Accountabilities include recruitment, drawing up rotas or keeping track of sales targets. The accountabilities were to replace traditional upwards promotion, which was no longer available under the flatter structure. The teams look after their own recruitment and promotion and the coach is available for training. The changes have meant that waitresses and chefs are now accountable for ordering their own stock, carrying out their own hygiene checks, dealing with customer complaints or cashing up. Four people are empowered as 'appointed people' to open up in the mornings and lock up at night.

Each team on each shift has a coordinator. All the team take it in turns to take on this role. It is a recognition that someone needs to make instant decisions. The staff are empowered to do virtually anything except decide whether they will be empowered. They also have tight targets to meet. Every waitress in the Dulwich branch is expected to sell a side order to every table. If they do not do this the team want to know what went wrong.

Every restaurant in the chain is run in the same way. Competition is encouraged between restaurants and a bonus system operates at that level (for the whole team).

A good example of team decision making is that one restaurant in a tourist area was so seasonal that staff decided to give up summer holidays altogether and take them in the winter.

A Training Workshop

Training is a key tool for introducing and maintaining change in the organisation. If the change is to create an empowered organisation then the training activity will have to support that. The following details are from a workshop developed by JRK Consultants as part of an empowerment programme. The workshop has been designed to teach general and supervisory staff some of the basic skills they will require if they are to take on additional responsibility and be more effective in their jobs. Where I have run this workshop I have dovetailed it with assertiveness skills (see Chapter 8), as assertiveness is another key skill that all staff will need.

COMMUNICATION & INFLUENCING SKILLS WORKSHOP
A workshop to help you improve your Communication skills and achieve results through others

Workshop Objectives

Having attended this workshop, participants will:

- Be more effective in their dealings with peers, subordinates, superiors and customers.
- Be able to appreciate the inherent differences between individuals.

- Have developed a range of influencing styles, as appropriate for different situations.
- Be able to give appropriate feedback.

Course Content

- Questioning and listening skills.
- Understanding and managing differences.
- Styles and strategies for influencing other people.
- Giving feedback to other people (in the form of praise or criticism).
- Developing strategies for putting the skills into practice.

Who Should Attend

- Anyone who needs to increase the influence they have on other people to achieve results.
- Anyone who has difficulty influencing other individuals or groups.
- Individuals who need to revise or develop their core interpersonal skills of questioning, listening, and giving appropriate feedback.

Course Style

- The workshop will be highly participative. Delegates will be expected to share experiences and participate in discussions. Delegates will be expected to participate in a variety of learning activities, an example of which will be 'The Lego Challenge' where delegates will work in small groups on their questioning and listening skills.

MANAGERS' BRIEF FOR
COMMUNICATION AND INFLUENCING SKILLS WORKSHOP

Workshop Objectives

The workshop has been designed to develop the basic interpersonal communication skills required by individuals in 'flatter' organisations.

The skills are essential to making the human resource more effective and efficient by enabling individuals to be more successful in their dealings with others, whether superiors, peers, subordinates or customers.

The workshop consists of four modules:

- Unit 1: Communication Skills
- Unit 2: Understanding and Managing Differences
- Unit 3: Influencing Skills
- Unit 4: Giving Appropriate Feedback

Workshop Content

Unit 1: Communication Skills

These are essential skills required to clarify what is expected of an individual. By using exercises such as 'The Lego challenge' it is possible to highlight to delegates how vital these skills are to achieving tasks quickly and successfully.

This unit consists of work on listening skills and questioning. The unit ends with an exercise to highlight the skills. The usual exercise is for the group to reproduce a model that is out of sight for all the group except one person. This is a very difficult task and great attention is required in both listening and questioning.

Unit 2: Understanding and Managing Differences

This part of the workshop is devoted to appreciating that individuals are different. They have different perceptions and values. Therefore, for delegates to be successful in their dealings with other people they have to recognise these different viewpoints.

This unit concentrates on a basic understanding of personality and individual differences. We would look at perception, values and prejudices. An exercise for this unit is a 'balloon debate'. Delegates are given a situation and brief resumés of the individuals involved. They have to come up with an 'order' in which the people are to be saved. (Although I have some reservations about the morality of such exercises they do help delegates to think about valuing differences.)

Unit 3: Influencing Skills

Individuals will have a chance to look at a range of influencing skills, see what their predominant style is and explore other styles. The styles highlighted are: rewards and punishments, participation and trust, common vision and assertiveness.

A simple questionnaire is used to help delegates understand their preferred style of influencing others. This exercise helps delegates to think about how effective they are currently and gives them the opportunity to think about, and try, other styles. As with the other units group interaction and discussion is very important here as delegates can obtain feedback from their peers on how they come across. There is often a gap between what they intend and the effect that this has.

Unit 4: Giving Appropriate Feedback

A key area for achieving results through other people is that of giving appropriate feedback. Delegates will learn about giving motivational (positive) feedback and when and how to give formative feedback, the feedback for how to change or modify behaviours.

If employees are to be empowered, and through assertiveness training to be able to ask for what they want, it is important that they are able to provide useful and relevant feedback. The workshop is designed to spend some time looking at formative and motivational feedback.

All the units are brought together in a final role-playing exercise where delegates can practise and rehearse situations that they find difficult.

Bibliography

Adair, J. (1973) *Action-Centred Leadership*, Gower.

Alliance & Leicester (1989) *Personnel Management*, Sept.

Armstrong, M. (1991) *A Handbook of Personnel Management Practice*, 4th edn, Kogan Page.

Beckhard, R. (1969) *Organization Development*, Addison-Wesley.

Belbin, M. (1981) *Management Teams: Why They Succeed or Fail*, Heinemann.

Berne, E. (1964) *Games People Play*, Grove Press.

Bevan, S. and Thompson, M. (1991) 'Performance Management at the Cross Roads, *Personnel Management*, Nov.

Blake, R. and McCanse, A.A. (1991) *Leadership Dilemmas. Grid Solutions*, Gulf Publishing.

Burns, T. and Stalker, G. (1966) *The Management Innovation*, Tavistock.

Carlzon, J. (1978) *Moments of Truth*, Harper & Row.

Cattell, R.B. (1963) *The 16 Personality Factor Questionnaire*, IPAT.

Child, J. (1979) *Organisation*, Harper & Row.

Clarke, C. and Pratt, S. (1985) 'Leadership's Four-Part Progress', *Management Today*, March.

Cole, G.A. (1990) *Management Theory and Practice*, 3rd edn, DP Publications.

Cooper, C. (1990) *The Sunday Times*, 18 February 1990.

Crosby, P. (1978) *Quality is Free*, McGraw-Hill.

Drucker, P. (1955) *The Practice of Management*, Heinemann.

Drucker, P. (1974) 'New Templates for Today's Organizations', *Harvard Business Review*, Jan/Feb.

Egan, G. (1975) *The Skilled Helper*, Wadsworth.

Eysenck, H. (1965) *The Structure of Human Personality*, Penguin.

Fayol, H. (1949) *General and Industrial Management*, trans. Constance Storrs, Pitman.

Fiedler, F. (1967) *A Theory of Leadership Effectiveness*, McGraw-Hill.

Fitts, P. (1965) 'Factors in Complex Skill Training' in Glaser, R. (ed), *Training and Education Research*, (John Wiley).

Fox, A. (1966) *Industrial Sociology and Industrial Relations*, HMSO.

Fraser, J.M. (1958) *A Handbook of Employment Interviewing*, MacDonald & Evans.

French, J. and Raven, B. (1953) 'The Bases of Social Power' in Cartwright, D. and Zander, A. (eds), *Group Dynamics*, Harper & Row.

Friedman M. and Rosenman, R. (1974) *Type A Behaviour and Your Heart*, Knopf.

Goldthorpe, J.H. *et al.* (1968) *The Affluent Worker*, Cambridge University Press.

Gray and Starke (1988) *Organisation Behaviour: Concepts and Applications*, 4th edn, Penguin.

Hamblin, A.C. (1974) *Evaluation and Control of Training*, McGraw-Hill.
Handy, C. (1991) *The Age of Unreason*, 2nd edn, Random House.
Handy, C. (1987) *Understanding Organisations*, 3rd edn, Penguin.
Harrison, R. (1972) 'How to Describe your Organisation', *Harvard Business Review*, Sept/Oct.
Harvey-Jones, Sir J. (1984) RSA Centaur Lecture.
Hertzberg, F., Mausner, B. and Snyderman, B. (1959) *The Motivation to Work*, John Wiley.
Hogg, C. (1988) *Performance Appraisal*, Factsheet 3, Institute of Personnel Management, March.
Honey, P. and Mumford, A. (1986) *A Manual of Learning Styles*, Honey.
Hopson, B. and Scally, M. (1991) *Twelve Steps to Success through Service*, Lifeskills.
Institute of Employment rights (1994) *Pay Equity – Just Wages for Women*.
Kirton, M. (1984) in Makin *et al.*, 'Adaptors and Innovators,' *Long Range Planning*, 17(2) pp. 137–143.
Kolb, D.A. (1984) *Experiential Learning,* Prentice-Hall.
Kotter, J. Schlesinger, L. and Sathe, V. (1986) *Organization: Text, Cases and Readings*, Irwin.
Lawrence, P. and Lorsch, J. (1967) *Organization and Environment*, Harvard University Press.
Longman Group UK Ltd (1991) *Developing Training Skills*, Longman.
Lowe, K. (1992) 'White Collar Tailoring', *Personnel Today*, 27 October.
Machiavelli (1513) *The Prince*, Penguin edn.
Makin, P. Cooper, C. and Cox, C. (1989) *Managing People at Work*, British Psychological Society.
Maslow, A. (1943) 'A Theory of Human Motivation', *Psychological Review*.
McGregor, D. (1957) 'An Uneasy Look at Performance Appraisal', *Harvard Business Review*, May/June.
McGregor, D. (1960) *The Human Side of Enterprise*, McGraw-Hill.
Megginson, D. and Boydell, T. (1984) *A Manager's Guide to Coaching*, BACIE (IPD).
Milgram, S. (1963) 'Behavioral Study of Obedience', *Journal of Abnormal Psychology*.
Mintzberg, W. (1973) *The Nature of Managerial Work*, Harper & Row.
Mullins, L.J. (1989) *Management and Organisational Behaviour*, 2nd edn, Pitman.
Munro Fraser, J.M. (1958) *A Handbook of Employment Interviewing*, MacDonald & Evans.
Nixon, B. and Pitts, G. (1991) 'W.H. Smith Develops a New Approach to Developing Senior Managers', *Industrial and Commercial Training*, vol. 23, no. 6.
Peter, L.J. (1985) *Why Things go Wrong*, Unwin Hyman.
Peters, T. and Austin, N. (1987) *A Passion for Excellence*, Macmillan.
Peters, T. and Waterman, R. (1982) *In Search of Excellence*, Harper & Row.
Pickard, J. (1993) 'Empowerment', *Personnel Management*, November.

Plato (1980) *The Republic*, Penguin edn.

Porter, L. and Lawler, E. (1968) 'What Job Attitudes Tell about Motivation', *Harvard Business Review,* Jan/Feb.

Porter, L., Lawler, E. and Hackman, J. (1975) *Behavior in Organizations*, McGraw-Hill.

Pym, D. (1986) 'Effective Managerial Performance in Organisational Change', *Journal of Management Studies*, vol. 3, no. 1.

Roethlisberger, F.J. and Dickson, W.J. (1939) *Management and the Worker*, Harvard University Press.

Rodger, A. (1952) *The Seven Point Plan*, National Institute of Industrial Psychology.

Schein, E. (1969) *Process Consultation*, Addison-Wesley.

Smith, M., Gregg, M. and Andrews, D. (1989) *Selection and Assessment: A New Approach*, Pitman.

Springsteen, B. (1989) taken from *Springsteen Live: The Boxed Set.*

Stewart, V. (1990) *David Solution: How to Reclaim Power and Liberate Your Organisation*, Gower.

Tannenbaum, R. and Schmidt, W. (1973) 'How to Choose a Leadership Pattern', *Harvard Business Review*, May/June.

Taylor, F.W. (1947) *Scientific Management*, Harper & Row.

Trist, E. (1963) *Organisational Choice*, Tavistock.

Tuckman, B.W. (1965) 'Development Sequence in Small Groups', *Psychological Bulletin*, vol. 63.

Vaughan, T.D. (1976) 'The Concept of Counselling' in *Concepts of Counselling*, Bedford Square Press.

Vroom, V.H. (1964) *Work and Motivation*, John Wiley.

Webster, E. (1964) *Decision Making in Employment Interviews*, McGill University Press.

Woodley, C. (1990) 'The Cafeteria Route to Compensation', *Personnel Management*, vol. 22, no. 5.

Woodward, J. (1965) *Industrial Organisation: Theory and Practice*, Oxford University Press.

Zaleznik, A. (1977) 'Manager and Leaders: Are They Different'? *Harvard Business Review*, May/June.

Index